ORIGAMI BY THE SEA

MARC KIRSCHENBAUM

FIT TO PRINT PUBLISHING, INC.
NEW YORK, NY

Origami by the Sea
Copyright © 2021
Fit To Print Publishing, Inc.

All rights reserved. No part of this publication may be reproduced, stored in a retrieval system or transmitted in any form or by any means, electronic, mechanical, photocopying, recording or otherwise, without the permission of the copyright holder.

ISBN 978-1-951146-17-7 (Paperback Edition)
ISBN 978-1-951146-18-4 (Hardcover Edition)

The diagrams in this book were produced with Macromedia's Freehand, and image processing was done with Adobe Photoshop. The Backtalk family of typefaces was used for the body text and the headers use Helvetica. Sants was used for the cover. Ellen Cohen assisted with the cover design and provided valuable artistic assistance. Special thanks to Sara Adams for providing some of the papers used.

Contents

Introduction	5
Paper & Materials	6
Symbols & Terminology	8
Seashell	14
Goldfish	16
Penguin	19
Angelfish	22
Koi	27
Clownfish	33
Dolphin	40
Snail	46
Shark	50
Walrus	59
Pelican	66
Whale	75
Lobster	84
Starfish	92
Crab	98
Seahorse	106
Octopus	115

Introduction

Our bodies of water harbor an amazing variety of creatures. This collection of origami pieces celebrates the diversity that lurks within and near our seas. There is a long history of sea life being depicted through folding paper, even going back to a few traditional forms. Asides from their novel beauty, these water-dwellers often sport intriguing symmetries and lots of appendages, making them fun challenges to origami designers.

Each of the seventeen origami pieces here raises that challenge by being foldable from commonly available six-inch (fifteen centimeter) origami papers. Typically, with models having many appendages, the resulting fold is very thick to accommodate the way layers of paper need to traverse the perimeter of the flaps. A few of the pieces like the *Crab* and *Lobster*, have short appendages that give the illusion of length through connecting folded edges.

Other pieces like the *Goldfish* completely gloss over any anatomical detail. All are on the whimsical side, with some that can pass as cartoon characters, like the Pelican and *Whale*. Many fish have distinctive colorings, and pieces like the *Angelfish*, *Clownfish* and *Koi* depict these patterns through folding.

Although these sequences will not put too much strain on your paper, some of the folds might be challenging, especially to the novice folder. The *Octopus* has a series of tiny internal folds, but since they are hidden in the end, it is a forgiving model even if you deviate a bit with your accuracy. The *Dolphin* and *Seahorse* require sections to be inverted which might be daunting to some.

To ease you through, the models are roughly ordered by their difficulty level. If you find a particular sequence challenging, perhaps consider trying a larger paper to practice with. Also taking a break from folding can often work wonders. Most importantly, have fun recreating these works!

Paper & Materials

Picking the perfect paper for your origami project can range from fun to frustrating. There are many origami designs with well over a hundred steps that demand specialty papers that can handle their stressful folding sequences. Fortunately, all these simpler pieces can be made from almost any paper made for origami. While it might be tempting to just use copy paper (or any scrap paper lying around), often such materials are too thick to handle more than a few layers of folds.

One of the better varieties to consider is kami, which is the Japanese word for *paper*. It is often just simply sold as *origami paper*, being extremely common. It can be found on most online stores, hobby shops, and of course origami stores (such as The Source, which is part of OrigamiUSA). The standard size is six inches (or fifteen centimeters) which is suitable for these projects. You could also consider the larger ten-inch size (or twenty-five-centimeter variety).

Most kami papers sport a decorative side (either plain or patterned) with the other side being plain white. A few of the models showcase both sides of the paper, so you should consider the *duo* or *double-sided* variety of kami. Of course, stay clear from the papers that are simply the same color on both sides.

Other papers sold for origami purposes are not as easy to work with. Foil backed papers do look nice and shiny when they are pristine, but they will pick up any extraneous creases as you fold. Some sequences call for changing a valley fold to a mountain fold, and foil papers a notoriously inflexible at that task. Washi papers are typically very durable, but do not often hold a crease well without special treatment. One solution is to use glue while folding, with PVA adhesives being ideal.

More adventurous folders might consider custom paper preparations. This can be as simple as using a favorite giftwrap and cutting it down to size. If you are considering getting a paper cutter, rotary style is more accurate and far safer than the guillotine kind. A popular European wrapping paper variety is known as *kraft* paper, which is the German word for *strong*. Most origami shops will sell it precut into squares. Unfortunately, like most wrapping paper, it is plain on the other side. Some origami artists will paint their papers with watered down acrylic paints.

A less messy approach is to glue a lightweight sheet onto the other side. A perfect adhesive for this application is methylcellulose, often abbreviated as *MC*. MC comes in a powder form that needs to be mixed into cold water. About two teaspoons per 1.5 cups of water is a good ratio. After about thirty minutes of periodic stirring the MC will reach a syrupy consistency. It can be brushed on your paper (any cheap paintbrush is fine) after which you can place your thinner paper atop. You can then brush more MC for a better bond. The drying process can be accelerated with a table fan. Many of the models showcased here were prepared with this technique. Have fun experimenting with different materials.

Symbols & Terminology

Valley Fold

A dashed line with an open-headed arrow indicates to *Valley Fold* (fold forward in the direction of the arrow).

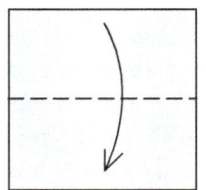 

1. Valley fold in half.　　2. Completed *Valley Fold*.

Mountain Fold

A dashed line with dots along with a closed-headed arrow indicates to *Mountain Fold* (fold behind in the direction of the arrow).

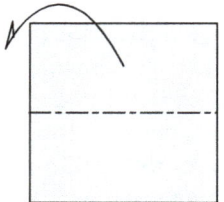 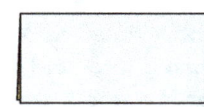

1. Mountain fold in half.　　2. Completed *Mountain Fold*.

Precrease

A valley fold line with a double-headed arrow indicates to Precrease (valley fold and then unfold in the direction of the open headed arrow). The resulting *crease* is represented by a thin line.

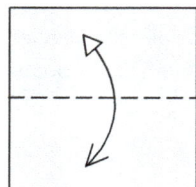 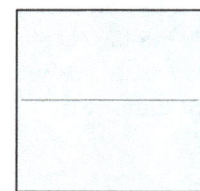

1. Precrease in half.　　2. Completed *Precrease*.

Turn Over

Turn over is indicated by a looped arrow.

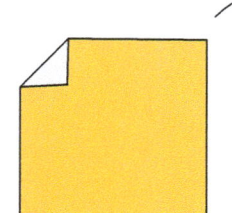 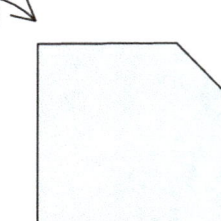

Rotate

Rotate is indicated by a circle with arrows along it.

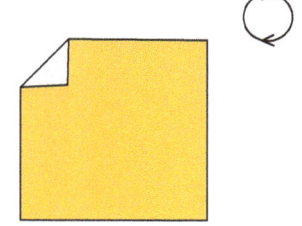

Hidden / Imaginary Lines

Hidden/Imaginary lines are indicated by a thin dotted line.

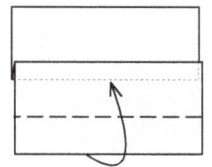 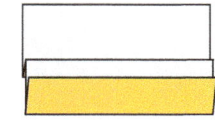

1. Valley fold to the hidden edge.
2. Completed fold.

Angle Bisectors

Open dots are sometimes used to indicate angle bisectors.

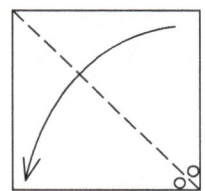 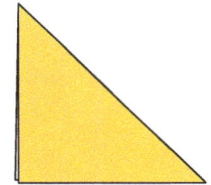

1. Valley fold along the indicated angle bisector.
2. Completed fold.

Divided Brackets

A divided bracket with tick marks shows equal divisions.

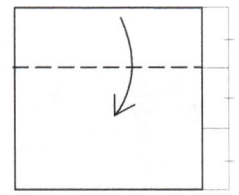 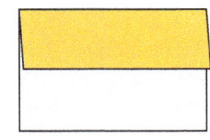

1. Valley fold along the 1/3rd mark.
2. Completed *Valley Fold*.

Reference Dots

Dots are sometimes used to call attention to a specific landmark.

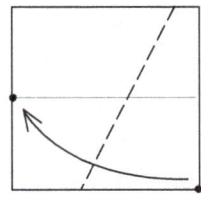 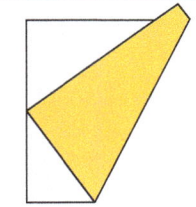

1. Valley fold the dotted corner to the dotted crease.
2. Completed fold.

Pleat Fold

A *Pleat Fold* is indicated by a mountain fold line followed by a valley fold line. An arrow indicates the direction of the pleat.

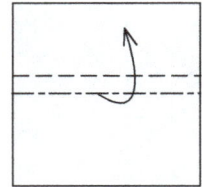 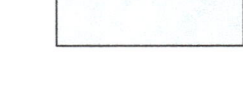

1. Pleat fold upwards. 2. Completed *Pleat Fold*.

Reverse Fold

A solid arrow indicates to push in or invert at the indicated area for a *Reverse Fold*, *Squash Fold* or various types of *Sink Folds*. For a *Reverse Fold*, you invert the indicated section.

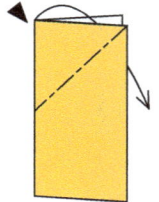 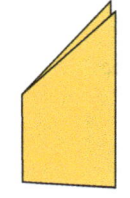

1. Reverse fold the corner. 2. Completed *Reverse Fold*.

Squash Fold

A *Squash Fold* is a combination of a reverse fold with opening out the inverted area.

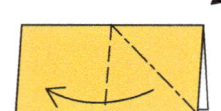 

1. Squash fold the corner. 2. Completed *Squash Fold*.

Sink Fold

A *Sink Fold* is related to a reverse fold, but it is performed on a point from the middle of the paper. After precreasing where this fold occurs, you open out the point and invert it along the perimeter of the creases.

1. Sink fold the corner. 2. Completed *Sink Fold*.

Closed Sink

Sink folds can also be formed without fully opening out the connecting layers. This is called a *Closed Sink*.

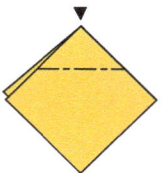 

1. Closed Sink fold the corner. 2. Completed *Closed Sink*.

Sink Triangularly

A hybrid version (half open and half closed) is called *Sinking Triangularly*.

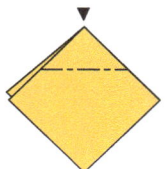 

1. Sink fold the corner triangularly.
2. Completed *Sink Fold*.

Petal Fold

A *Petal Fold* is indicated by an open headed arrow with squash fold arrows. A layer is raised up, causing side edges to get pulled inwards and squash folded flat.

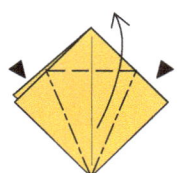 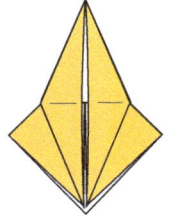

1. Petal fold the corner.
2. Completed *Petal Fold*.

Outside Reverse Fold

An *Outside Reverse Fold* is indicated by a set of arrows. You wrap around the indicated layer and flatten.

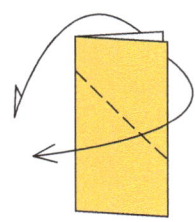 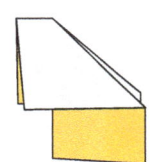

1. Outside reverse fold the corner.
2. Completed *Outside Reverse Fold*.

Crimp Fold

A *Crimp Fold* is indicated by a set of arrows. It is sometimes accompanied with a sink arrow or a set of zigzag lines to show how the layers are distributed. You spread apart the sides of a flap and form a set of valley and mountain folds on each side to change the position of the tip. There are a number of variations on this fold.

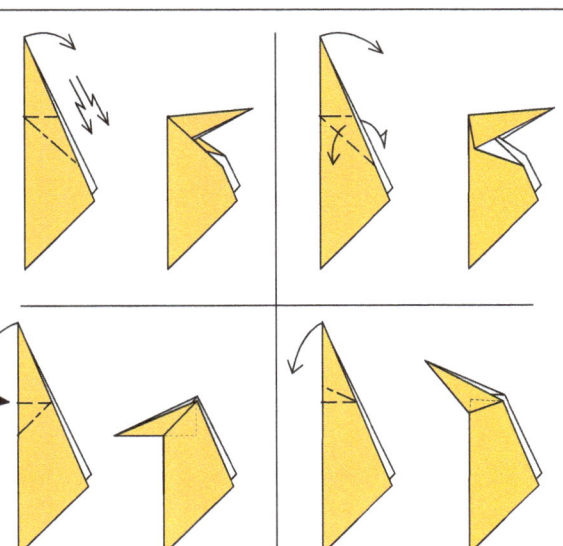

Spread Squash

A *Spread Squash* is a sink fold that is spread open.

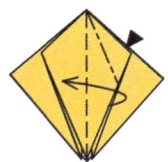 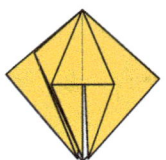

1. Spread squash the corner.
2. Completed *Spread Squash*.

Unsink

A hollow arrow is used to show an area to be unsunk or where layers would be pulled out.

 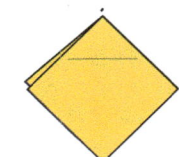

1. Unsink the corner.
2. Completed *Unsink*.

Swivel Fold

Swivel Fold is indicated by a set of arrows and sometimes accompanied with a sink arrow. Edges are folded over in two different areas, while the connecting paper is squash folded flat.

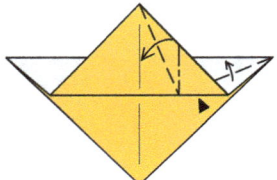 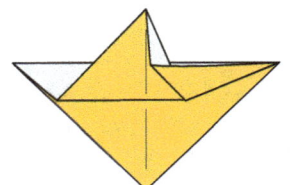

1. Swivel fold the corner.
2. Completed *Swivel Fold*.

Rabbit Ear

Rabbit Ear is indicated by a set of arrows. Two edges are valley folded in, while the connecting paper is pinched flat into a new flap.

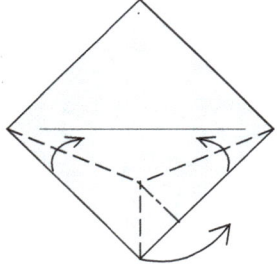 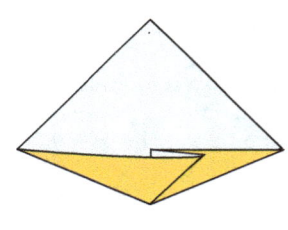

1. Rabbit ear the corner.
2. Completed *Rabbit Ear*.

Seashell

seashell

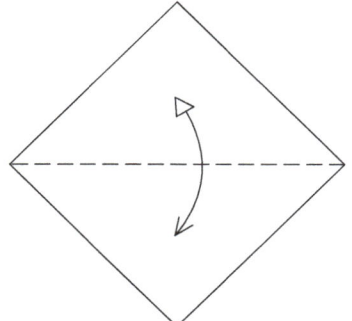

1. Precrease along the diagonal.

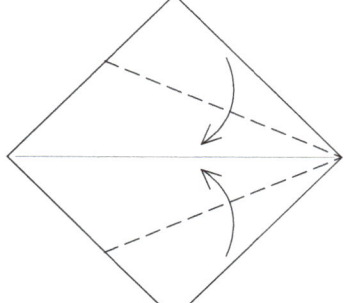

2. Valley fold the sides to the center.

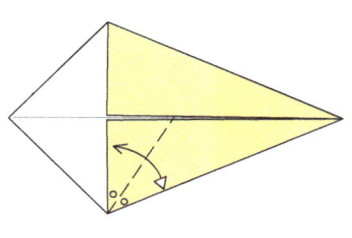

3. Precrease along the indicated angle bisector.

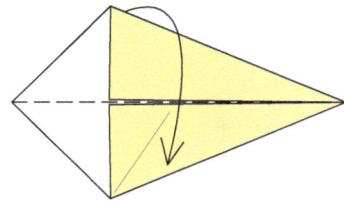

4. Valley fold in half.

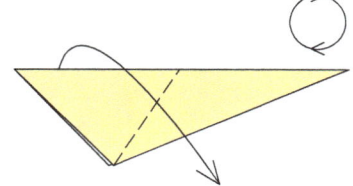

5. Valley fold using the hidden crease as a guide. Rotate the model slightly.

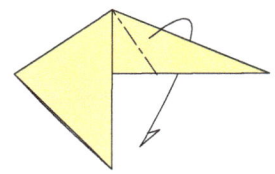

6. Mountain fold the flap down.

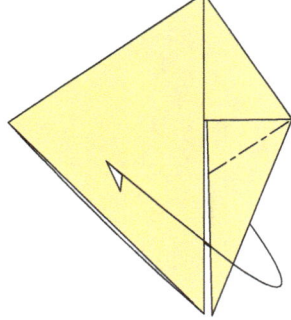

7. Mountain fold the flap, allowing its tip to lay on the surface.

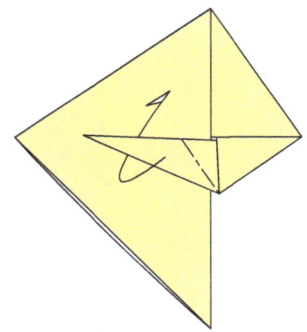

8. Mountain fold the flap again.

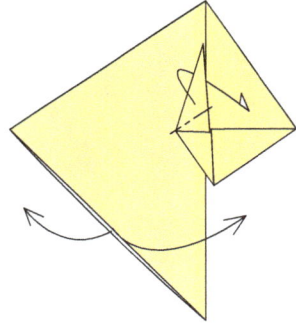

9. Mountain fold the flap one more time. Open out the bottom slightly.

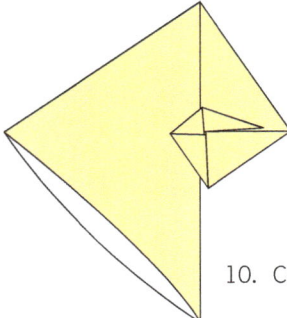

10. Completed *Seashell*.

15

Goldfish

g o l d f i s h

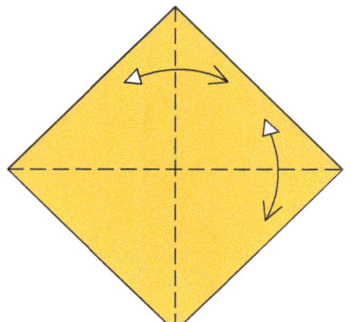 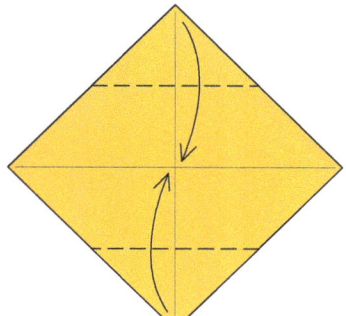 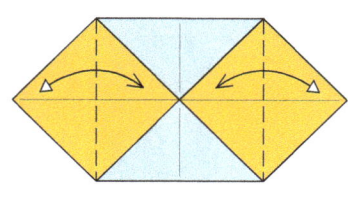

1. Precrease along the diagonals.
2. Valley fold the corners to the center.
3. Precrease the sides to the center.

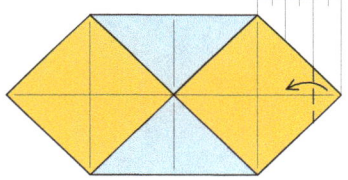 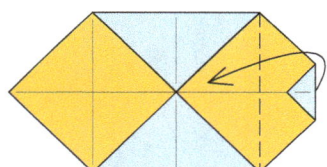 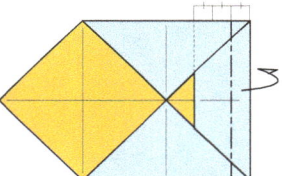

4. Valley fold the corner in about 1/3rd the width.
5. Valley fold the side in.
6. Mountain fold the side in about 1/3rd the width.

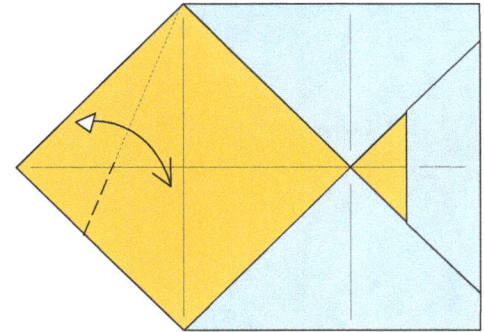 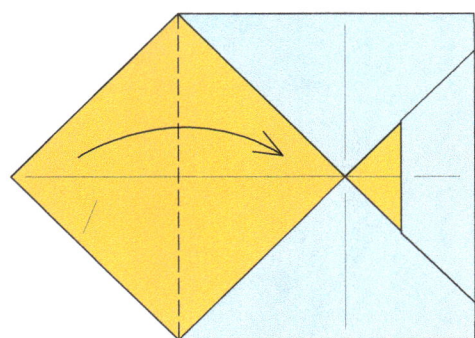

7. Pinch the edge along the indicated angle bisector.
8. Valley fold the side in.

17

goldfish

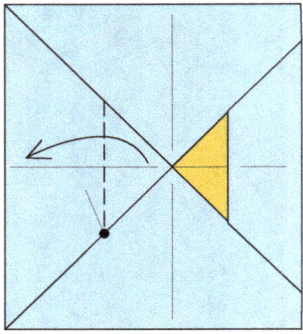

9. Valley fold the corner outwards starting from the dotted intersection.

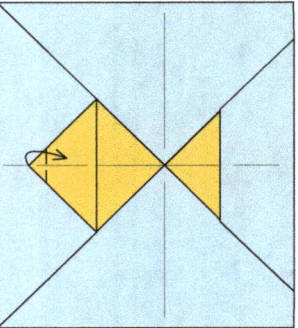

10. Valley fold the tip of the flap inwards.

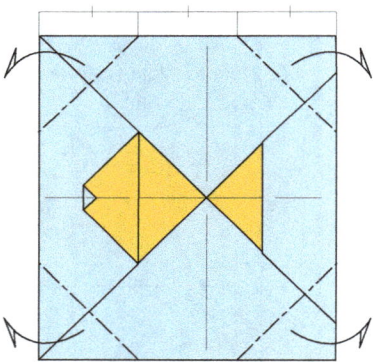

11. Mountain fold the corners behind.

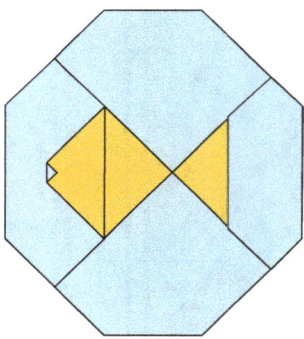

12. Completed *Goldfish*.

Penguin

penguin

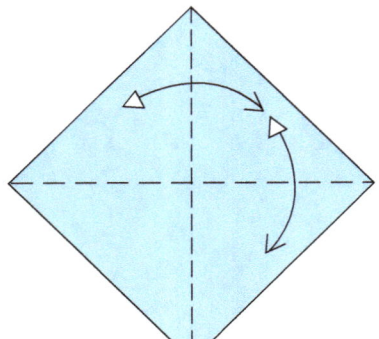
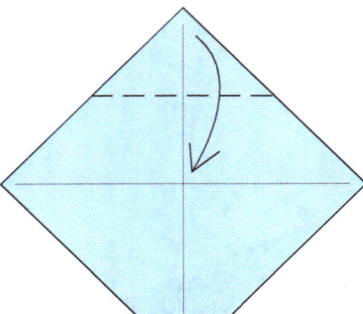
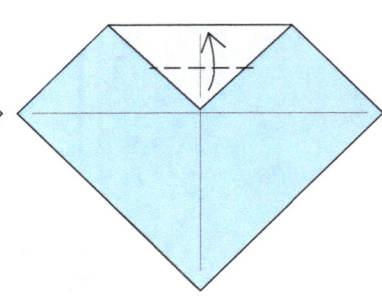

1. Precrease along the diagonals.

2. Valley fold to the center.

3. Valley fold up to the top edge.

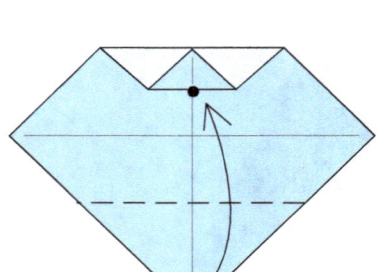
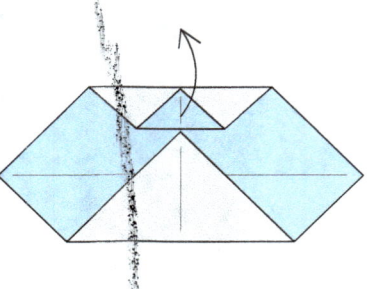
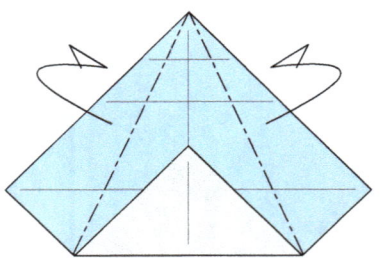

4. Valley fold to the dotted intersection.

5. Unfold the top pleat.

6. Mountain fold the sides behind. The edges will *not* meet at the center.

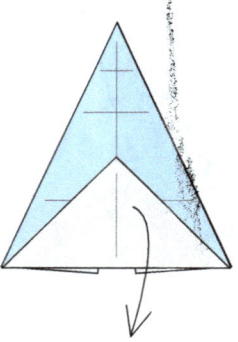
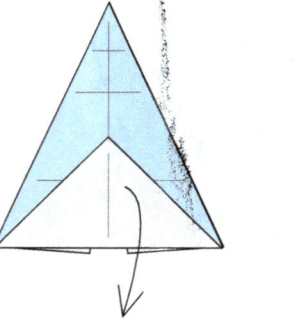
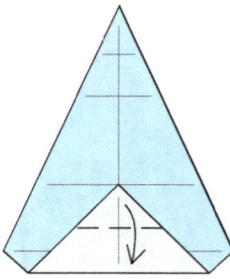

7. Swing the flap down.

8. Valley fold to the dotted intersection.

9. Valley fold towards the bottom edge.

penguin

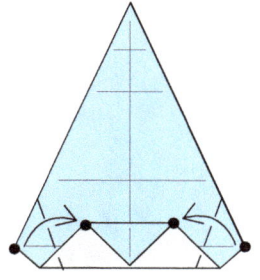

10. Valley fold the sides towards the dotted corners.

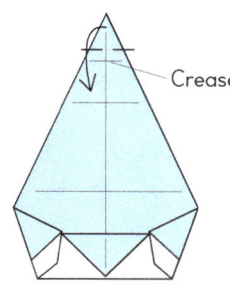

11. Valley fold down, starting a little bit above crease A.

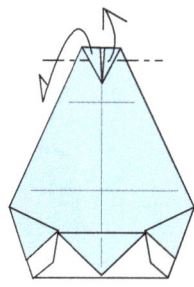

12. Mountain fold along crease A, allowing the flap to flip behind.

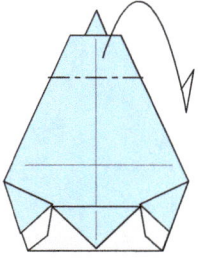

13. Mountain fold along the existing crease.

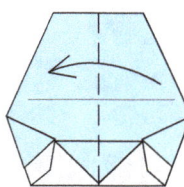

14. Valley fold in half.

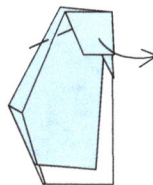

15 Slide the head outwards.

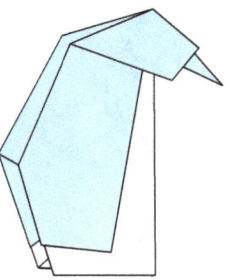

16. Completed *Penguin*.

Angelfish

angelfish

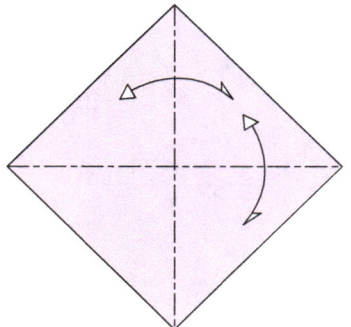

1. Precrease along the diagonals with mountain folds.

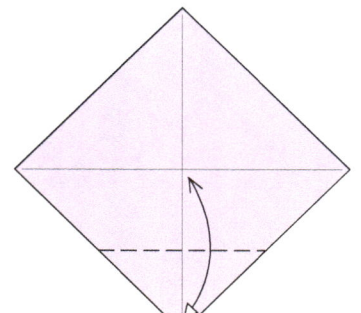

2. Precrease the corner to the center.

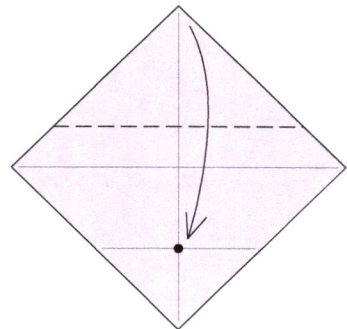

3. Valley fold the corner to the dotted intersection of creases.

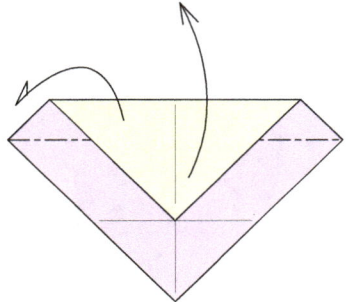

4. Mountain fold along the existing crease, allowing the front flap to flip up.

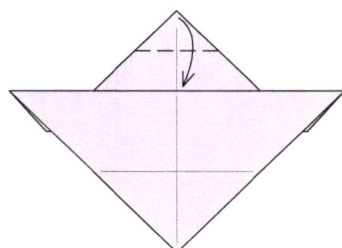

5. Valley fold the corner to the folded edge.

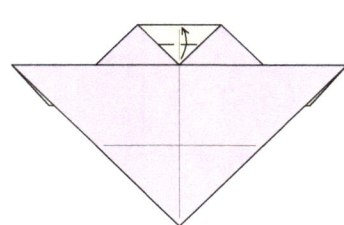

6. Valley fold the corner to the top.

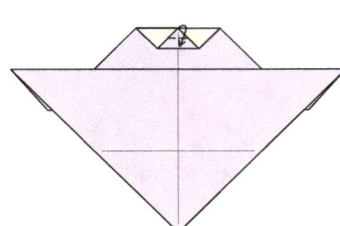

7. Valley fold the corner back down.

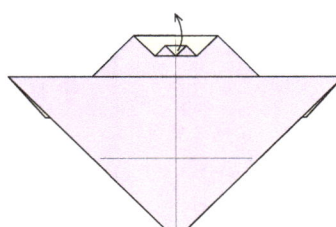

8. Unfold the top pleat.

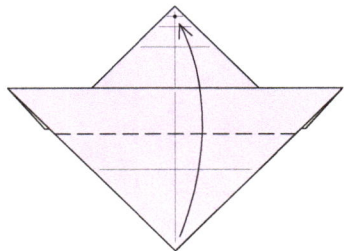

9. Valley fold to the dotted intersection of creases.

angelfish

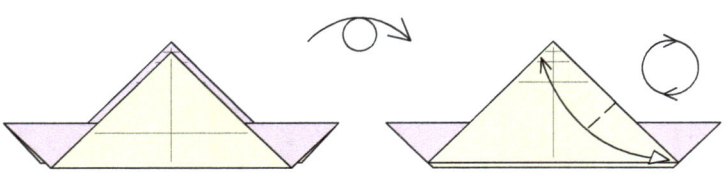

10. Turn over.

11. Precrease the side. Rotate the model.

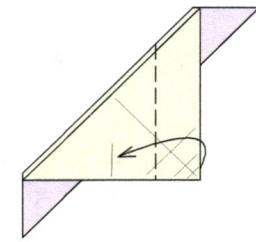

12. Valley fold the side edge to the crease.

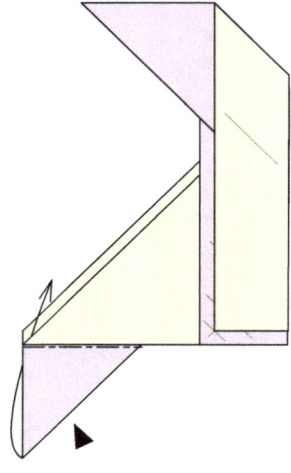

13. Reverse fold the corner up.

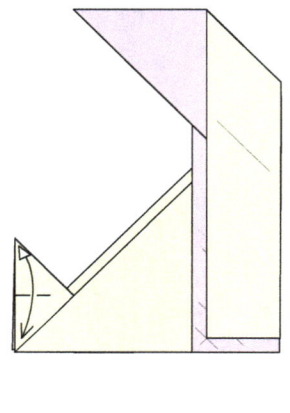

14. Precrease the flap in half.

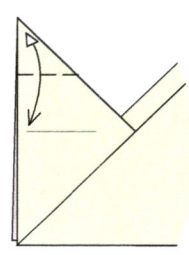

15. Precrease to the last crease.

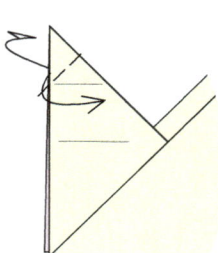

16. Outside reverse fold the corner.

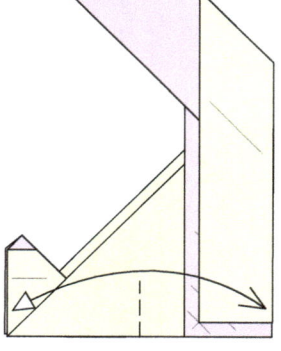

17. Precrease the bottom edge in half.

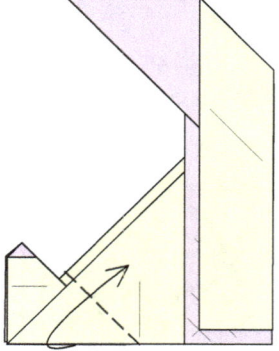

18. Valley fold to the last crease.

angelfish

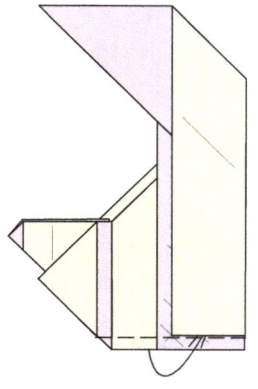

19. Valley fold the bottom edge up, tucking it into the pocket.

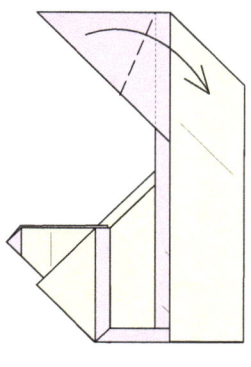

20. Valley fold the flap over so the edge lies straight.

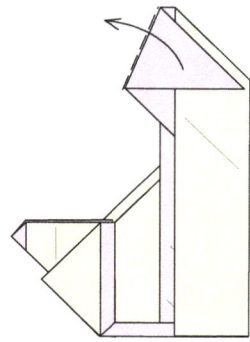

21. Open the flap back out.

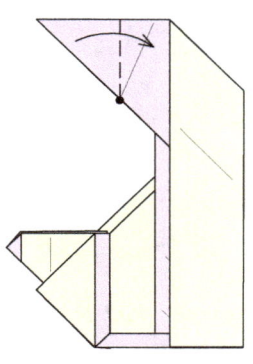

22. Valley fold over, starting from the dotted intersection.

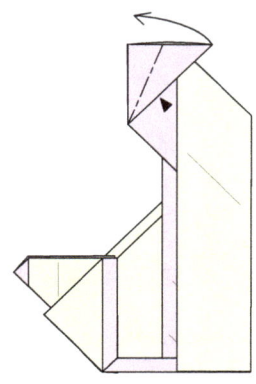

23. Squash fold the flap.

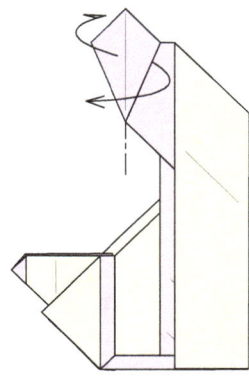

24. Flip the flap behind.

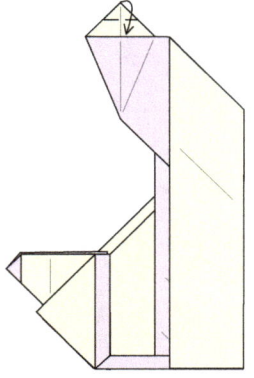

25. Valley fold the corner down.

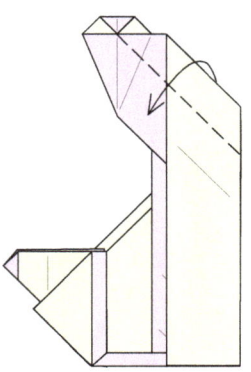

26. Valley fold the cluster of edges over.

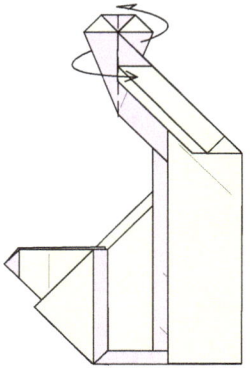

27. Flip the flap back to the front.

angelfish

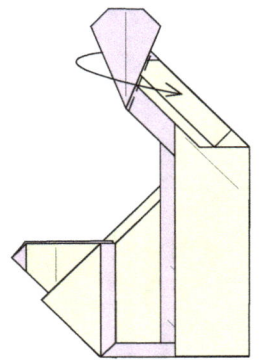

28. Valley fold the flap down.

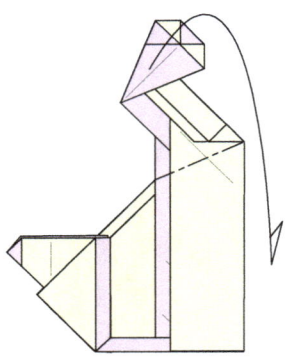

29. Mountain fold the top section behind.

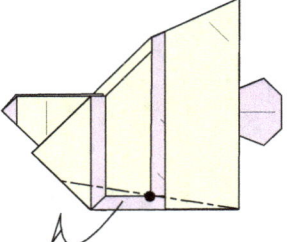

30. Mountain fold the bottom edge, passing through the dotted intersection.

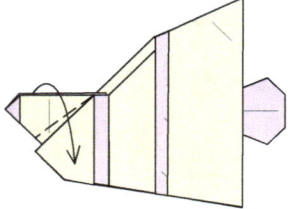

31. Valley fold the flap over, starting slightly above the folded edge.

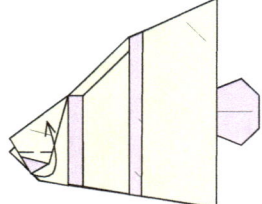

32. Valley fold the flap up.

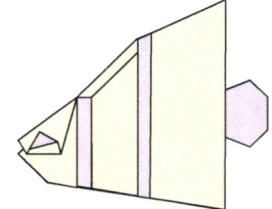

33. Completed *Angelfish*.

Koi

koi

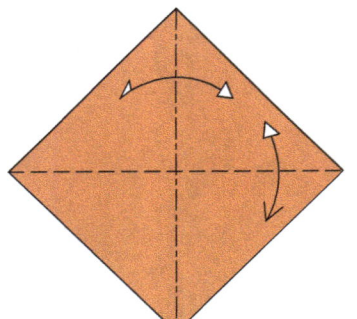

1. Precrease the diagonals with mountain and valley folds.

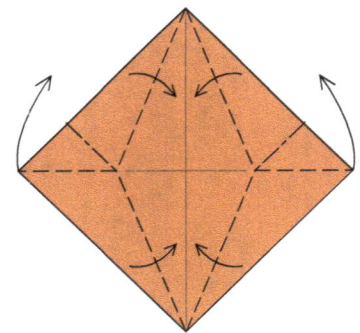

2. Rabbit ear the sides.

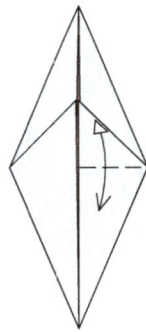

3. Precrease the flap.

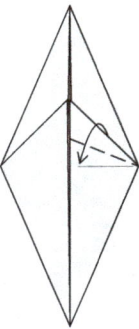

4. Valley fold along the angle bisector.

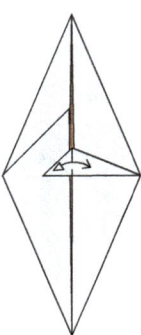

5. Precrease the tip of the flap.

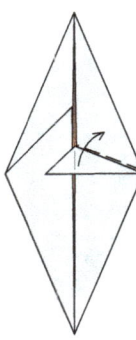

6. Open out the flap.

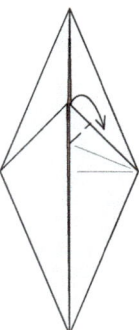

7. Outside reverse fold the tip of the flap along the existing crease.

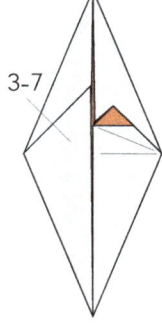

8. Repeat steps 3–7 in mirror image.

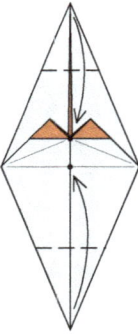

9. Valley fold towards the dotted intersections.

k o i

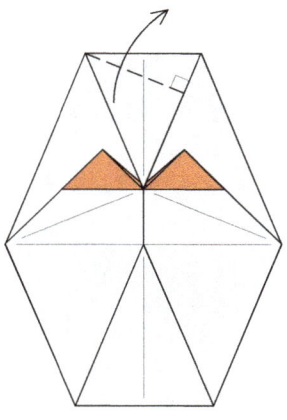

10. Valley fold the flap up, keeping the side edges aligned.

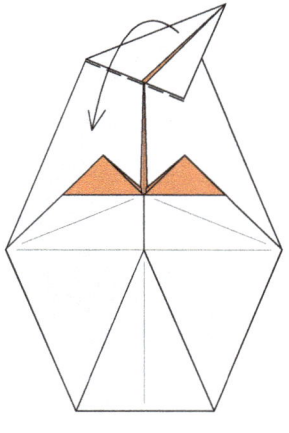

11. Swing the flap back down.

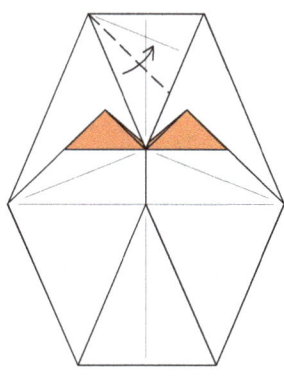

12. Valley fold towards the crease.

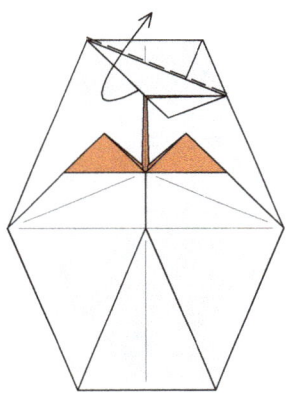

13. Pull around a single layer and flatten.

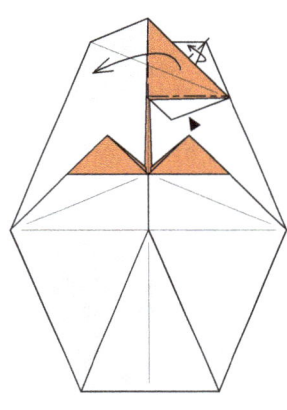

14. Squash the center flap over.

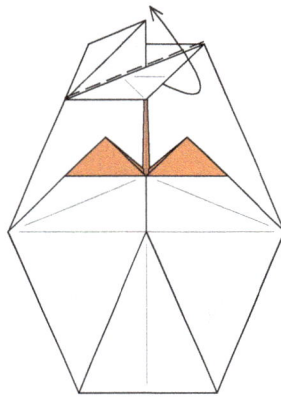

15. Pull around a single layer and flatten.

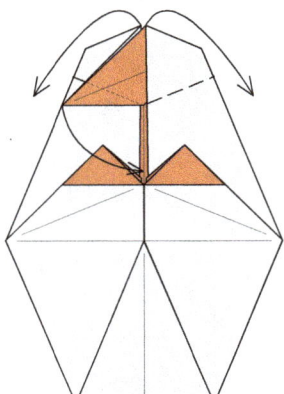

16. Spread open the top flaps and flatten.

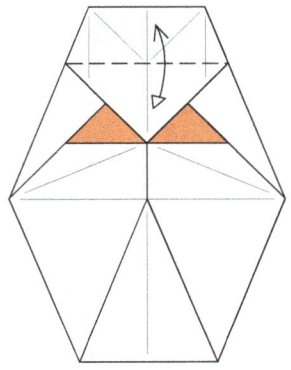

17. Precrease the top layer.

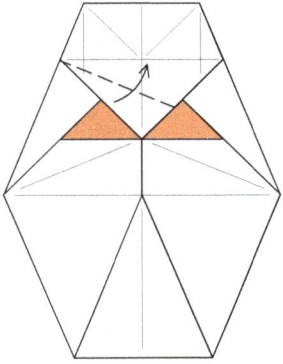

18. Valley fold to the crease.

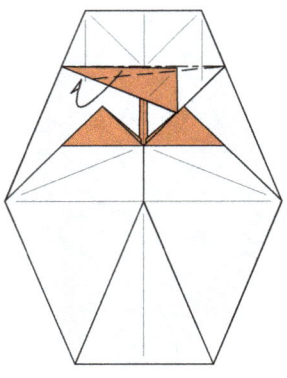

19. Pleat the bottom edge inside. There are no reference points for this fold.

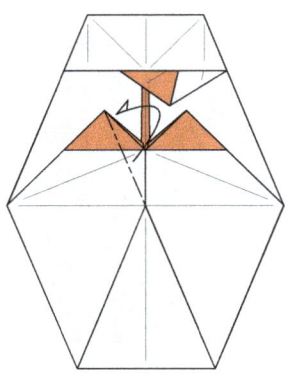

20. Mountain fold the corner behind.

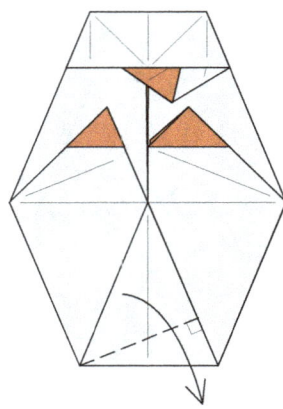

21. Valley fold the flap down, keeping the side edges aligned.

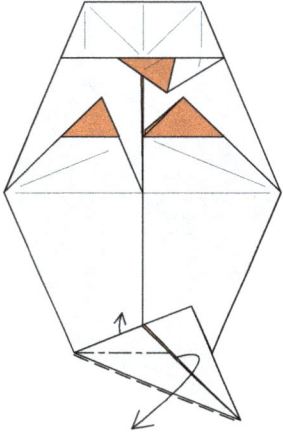

22. Pull out a single trapped layer and flatten.

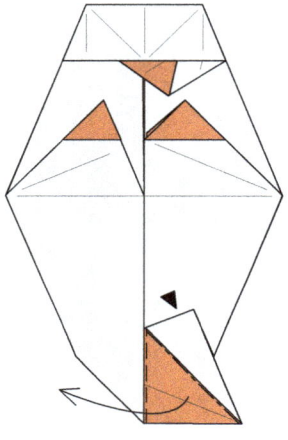

23. Squash the center flap over.

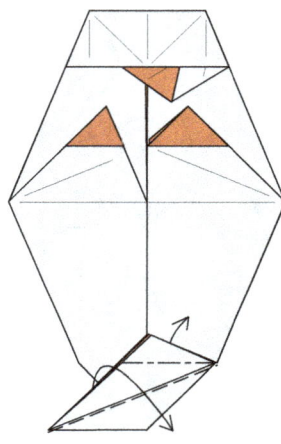

24. Pull out a single trapped layer and flatten.

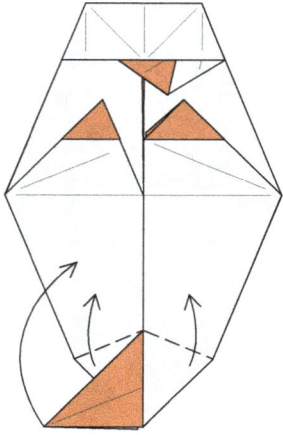

25. Spread open the bottom flaps and flatten.

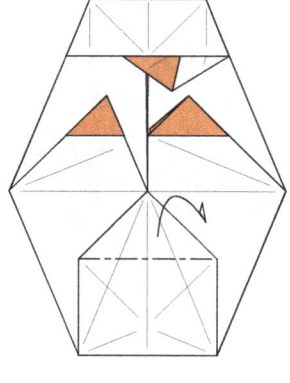

26. Mountain fold the flap inside.

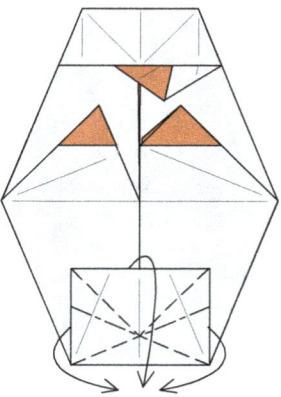

27. Swing the flap down while pleating the sides.

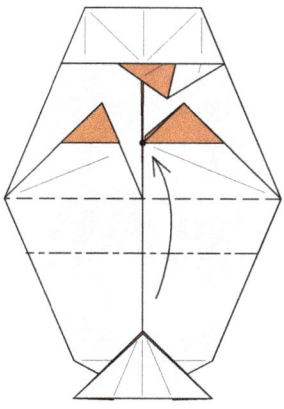 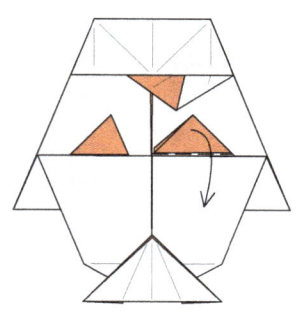 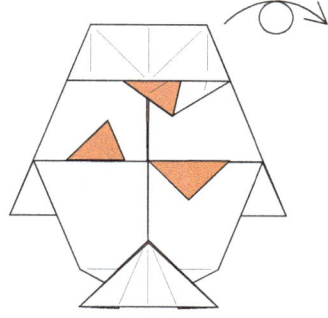

28. Pleat the bottom section to meet the dotted intersection.

29. Valley fold the flap down.

30. Turn over.

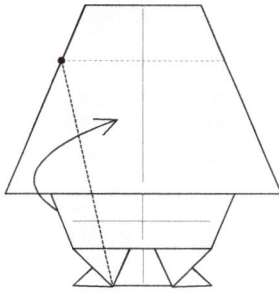 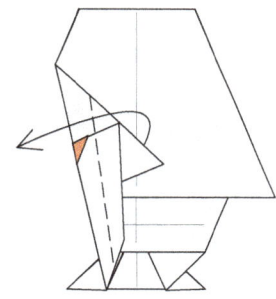 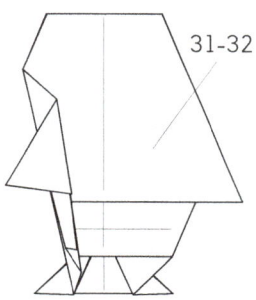

31. Valley fold the side inward, noting the dotted corner of the edge behind.

32. Valley fold towards the outer edge.

33. Repeat steps 31-32 in mirror image.

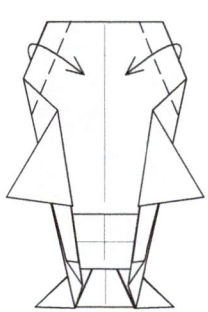  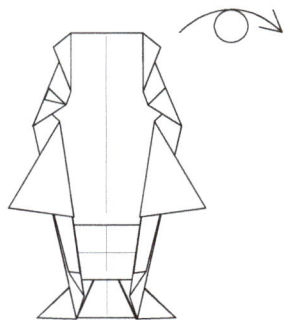

34. Valley fold the side edges inwards partway.

35. Valley fold the corners outwards.

36. Turn over.

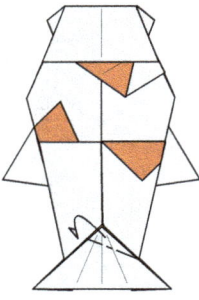

37. Mountain fold the corner inside.

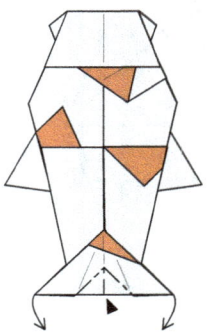

38. Push in the edge of the fins.

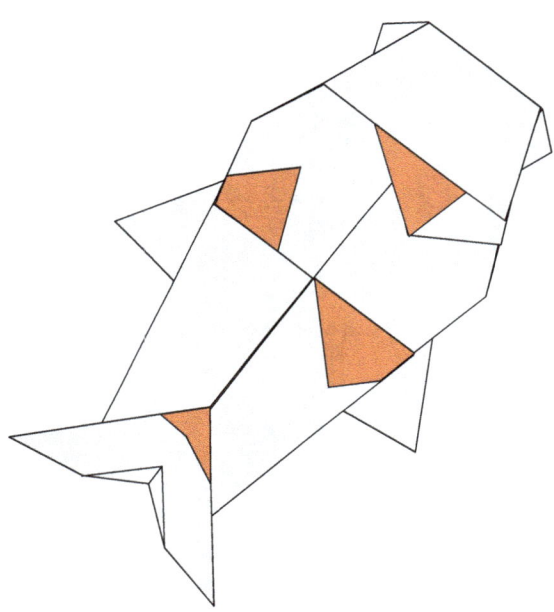

39. Completed *Koi*.

Clownfish

clownfish

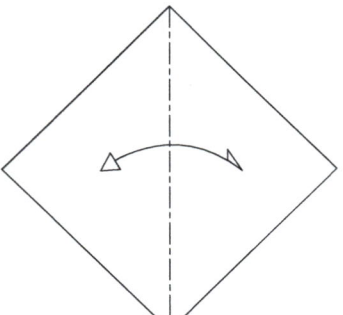

1. Precrease along the diagonal with a mountain fold..

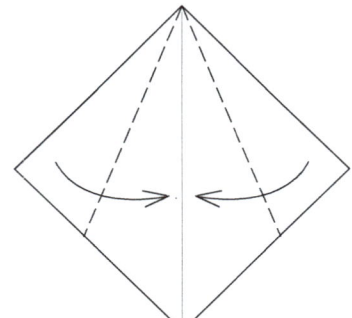

2. Valley fold the sides to the center.

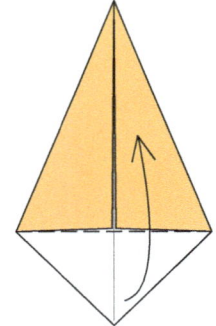

3. Valley fold the triangular flap up.

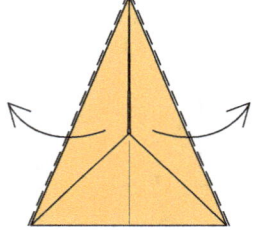

4. Open out the sides.

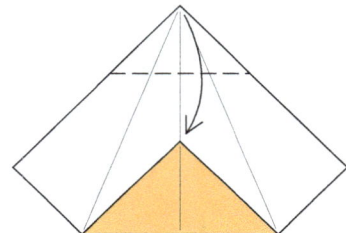

5. Valley fold to the corner.

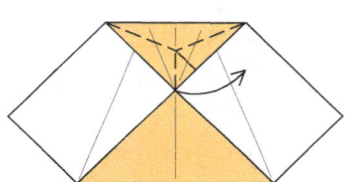

6. Rabbit ear the top flap.

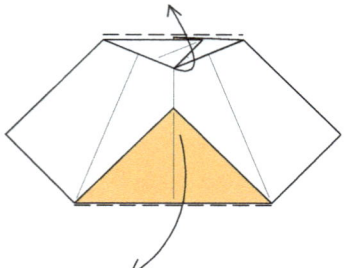

7. Swing the flaps outwards.

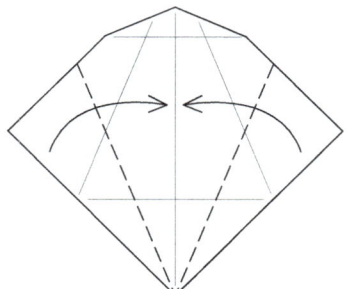

8. Valley fold the sides to the center.

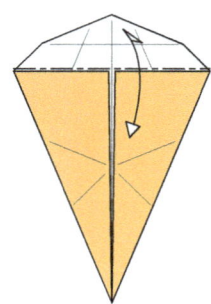

9. Precrease with a mountain fold.

clownfish

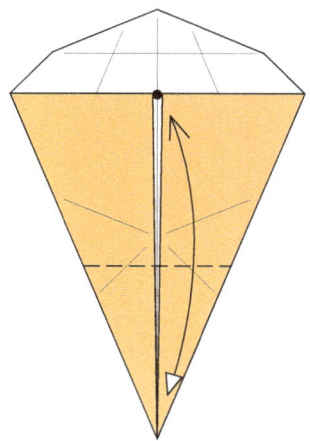

10. Precrease to the dotted corners.

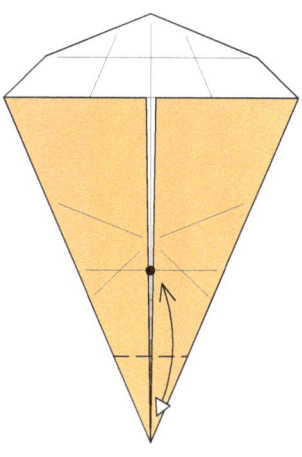

11. Valley fold to the dotted intersection.

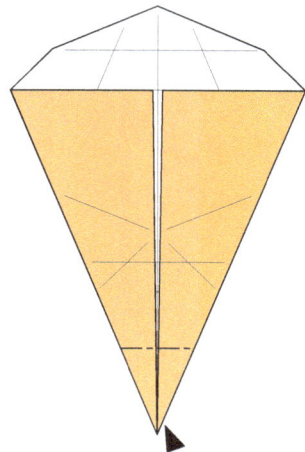

12. Reverse fold the flap along the existing crease.

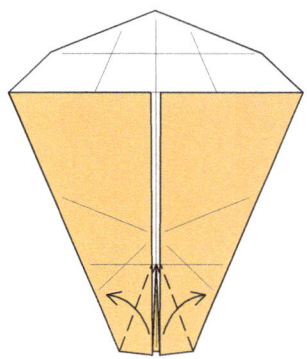

13. Valley fold the sides outwards.

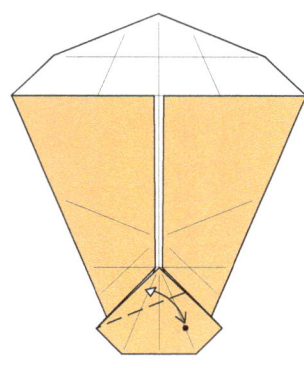

14. Precrease so the corner hits the dotted crease.

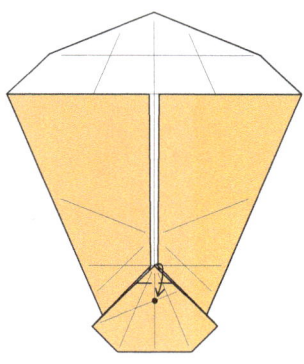

15. Valley fold to the dotted intersection of creases.

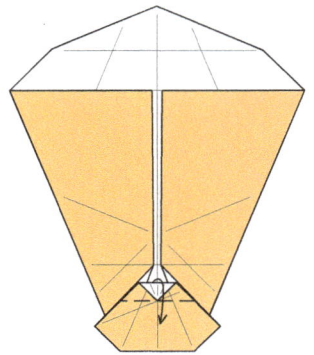

16. Valley fold down.

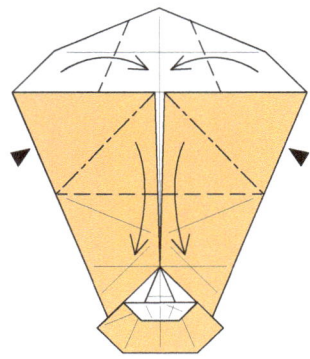

17. Swivel fold the flaps down.

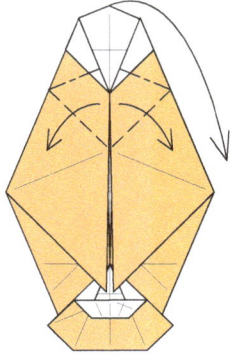

18. Valley fold the top layer along the existing creases, allowing the sides to squash fold outwards.

clownfish

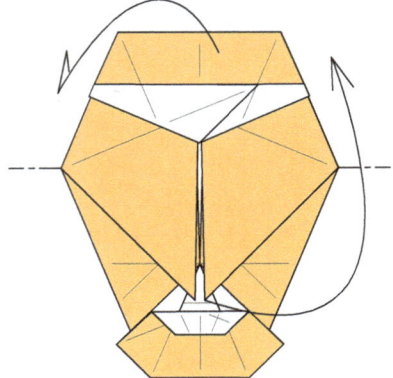

19. Swing the top section behind, allowing the center flaps to swing upwards.

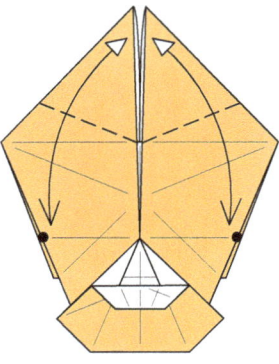

20. Precrease towards the dotted side intersections.

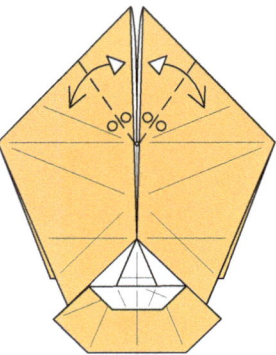

21. Precrease along the indicated angle bisectors.

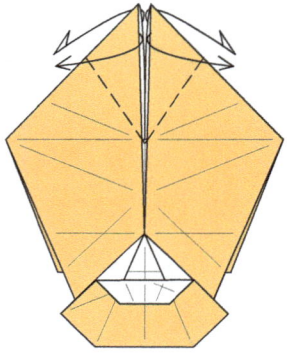

22. Outside reverse fold along the existing creases.

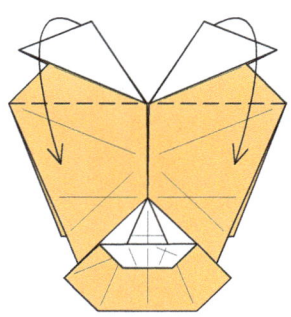

23. Valley fold the flaps down.

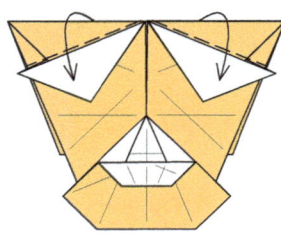

24. Valley fold the top edges down.

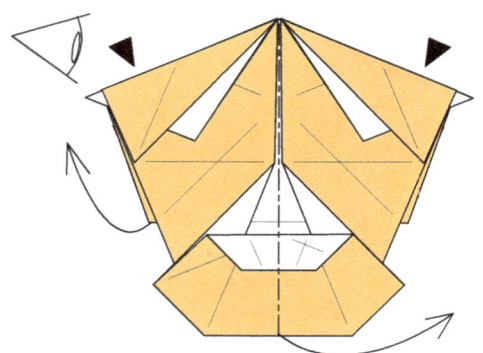

25. Push the sides in, allowing the front and back sections to flatten in half.

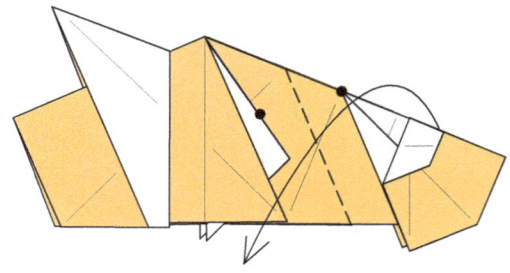

26. View from the previous step. Valley fold along the existing crease so the dotted points meet.

clownfish

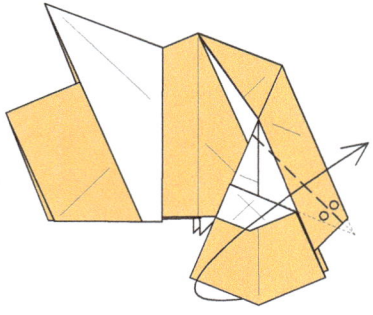

27. Valley fold along the indicated imaginary angle bisector.

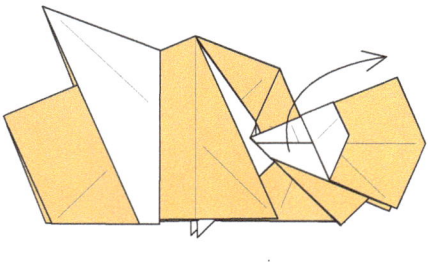

28. Unfold the pleat.

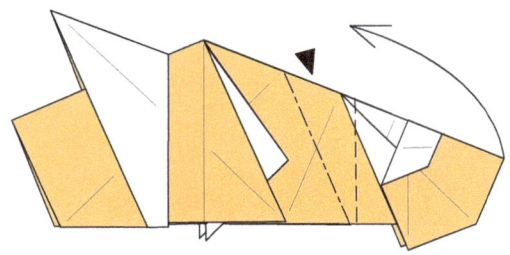

29. Reverse fold in and out along the existing creases.

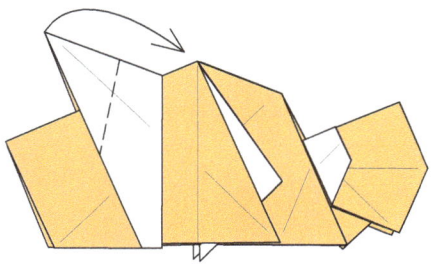

30. Outside reverse fold the flap.

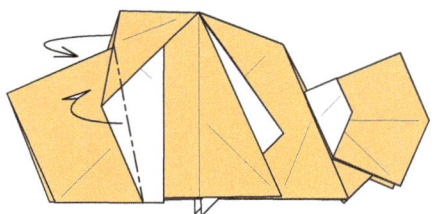

31. Mountain fold the edges inside at each side.

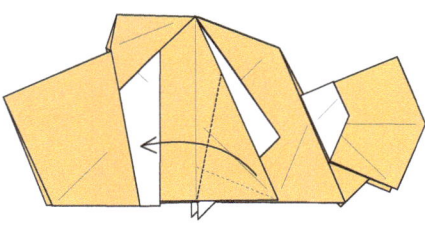

32. Valley fold so that the hidden edge lies straight.

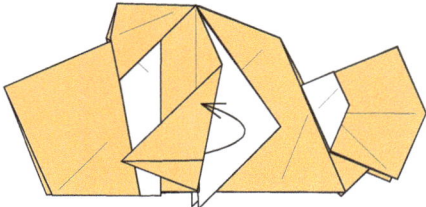

33. Tuck the flap into the pocket.

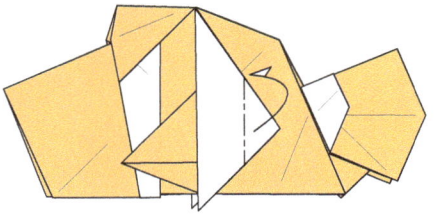

34. Mountain fold a little bit less than half the width of the flap.

clownfish

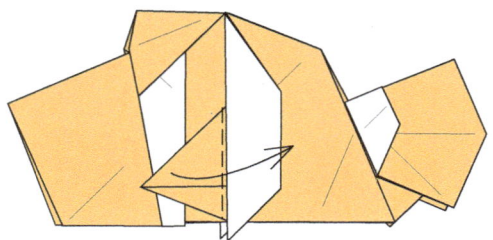

35. Valley fold the flap over.

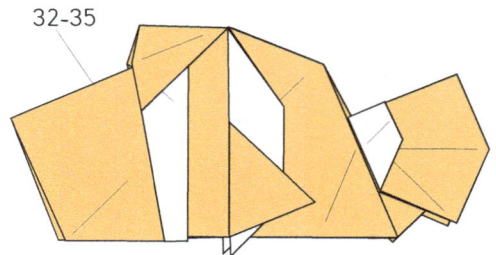

32-35

36. Repeat steps 32-35 behind.

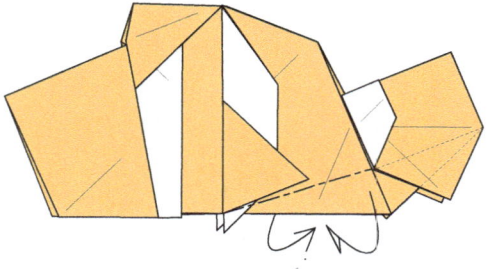

37. Mountain fold the bottom edges inside.

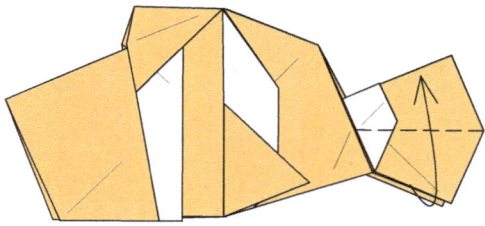

38. Lightly valley fold the top layer up.

39. Valley fold the two layers up together.

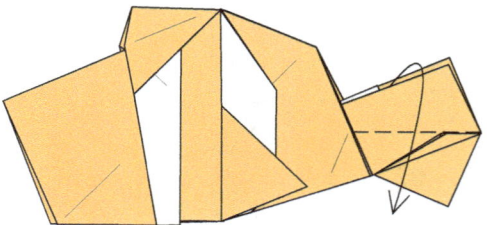

40. Swing the flap back down.

clownfish

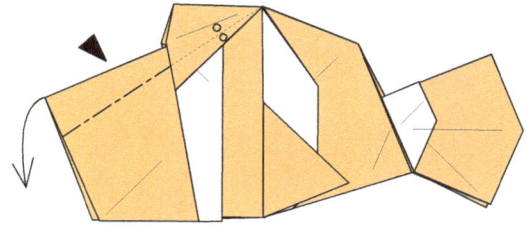

41. Reverse fold along the indicated angle bisector.

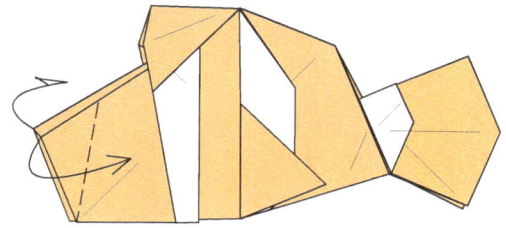

42. Valley fold the outer edges over as far as possible, starting from the bottom corner.

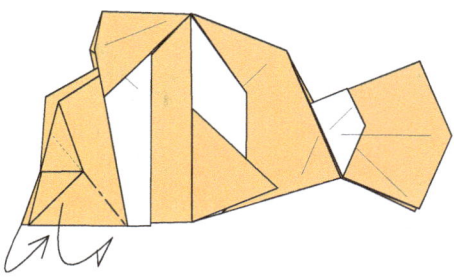

43. Mountain fold the bottom corners inside.

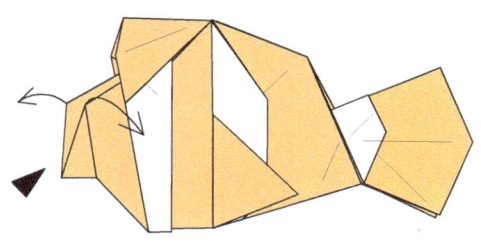

44. Spread apart the sides and flatten the corner.

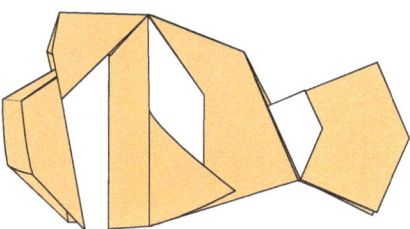

45. Completed *Clownfish*.

Dolphin

dolphin

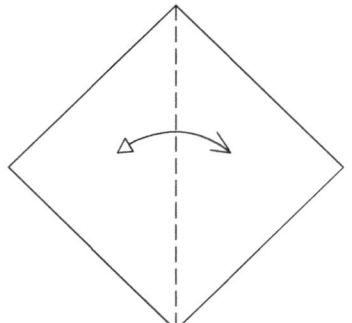

1. Precrease along the diagonal.

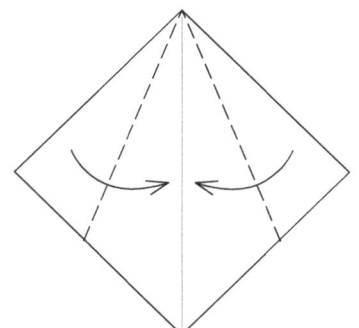

2. Valley fold to the center.

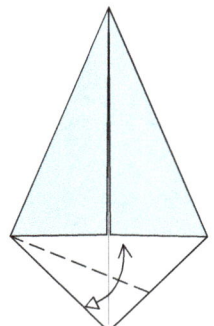

3. Precrease along the angle bisector.

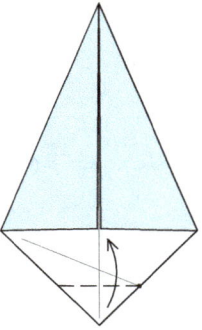

4. Valley fold up starting from the dotted intersection.

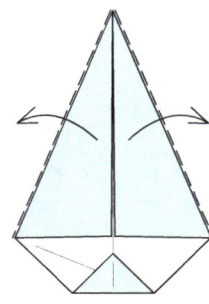

5. Open out the sides.

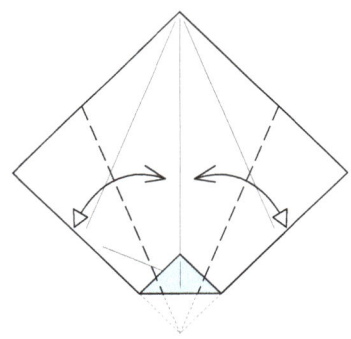

6. Precrease along the imaginary angle bisectors.

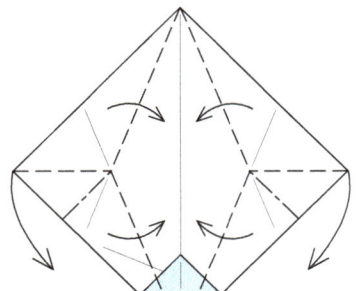

7. Rabbit ear the sides.

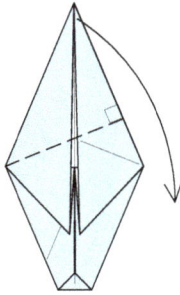

8. Valley fold down so the side edges are aligned.

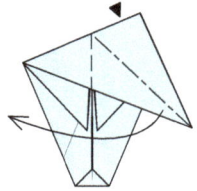

9. Squash fold the flap over.

dolphin

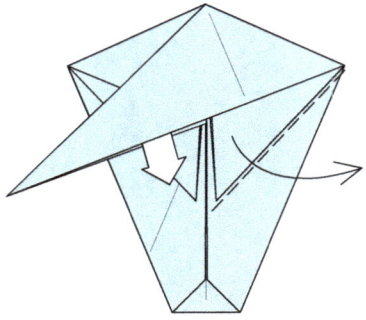 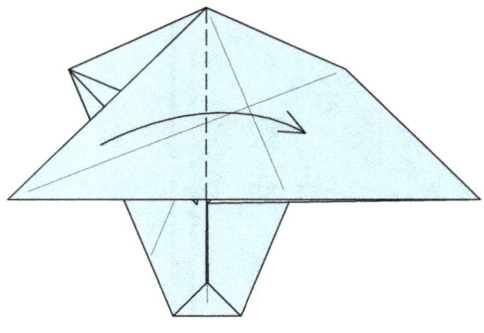

10. Slide the flap outwards, pulling out trapped paper from the center flap.

11. Valley fold the center flap over.

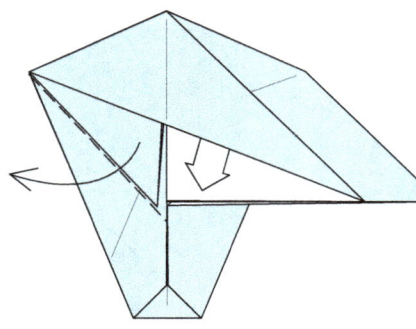 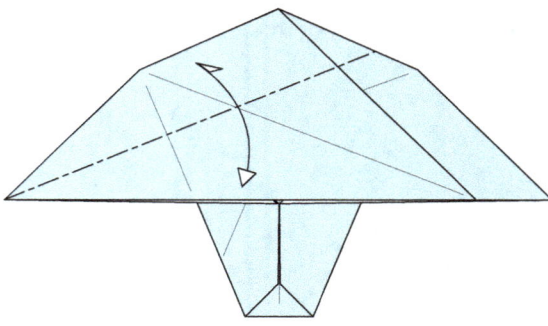

12. Slide the flap over while pulling out the trapped layer.

13. Precrease along the angle bisector with a mountain fold.

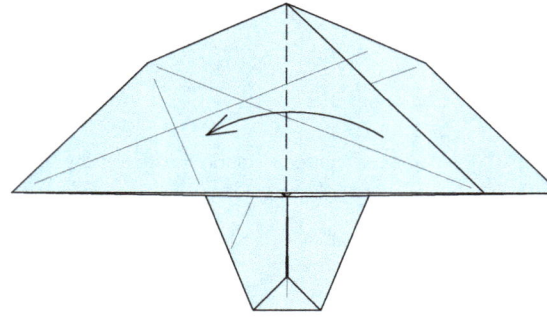 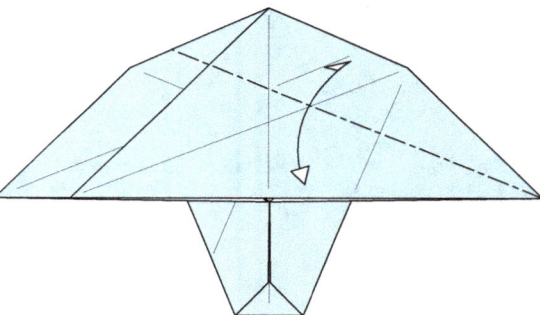

14. Swing the center flap over.

15. Precrease along the angle bisector with a mountain fold.

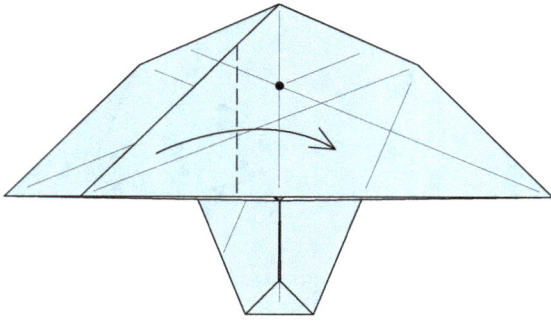 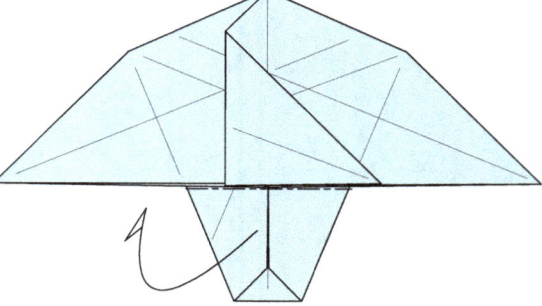

16. Valley fold the center flap over so it hits the dotted intersection of creases.

17. Mountain fold the bottom flap.

dolphin

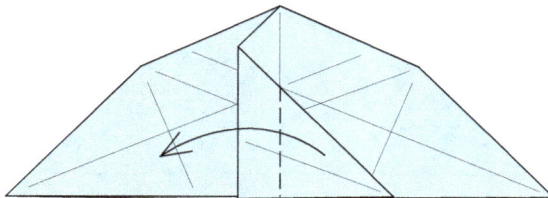

18. Valley fold, aligning along the center.

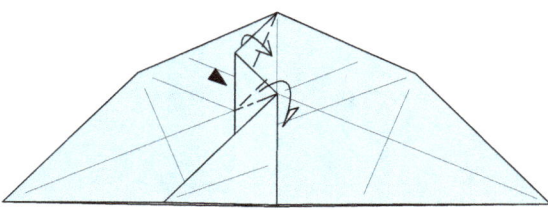

19. Valley fold along the angle bisector, swivel folding the excess paper behind.

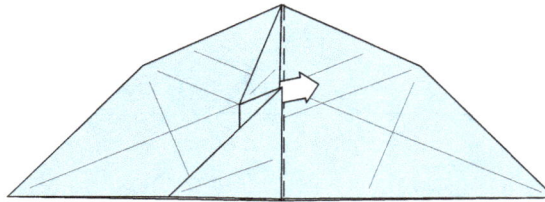

20. Pull out a single layer and collapse it flat to match the other side.

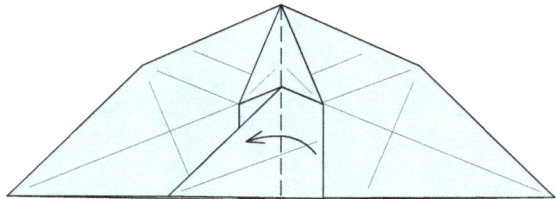

21. Swing over one flap.

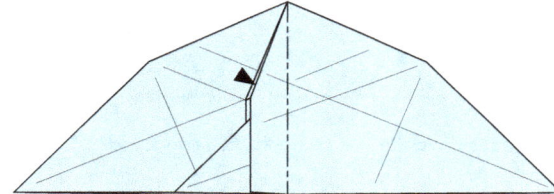

22. Reverse fold the flap through.

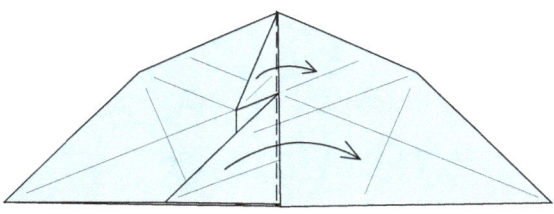

23. Swing over two flaps.

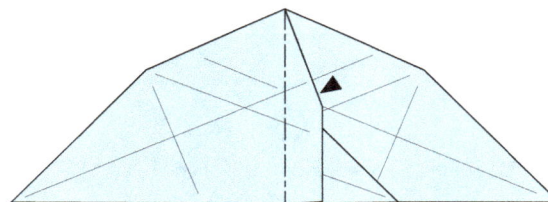

24. Reverse fold the flap through.

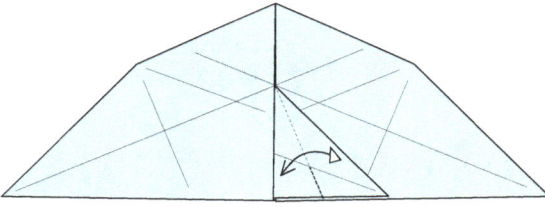

25. Pinch the bottom edge along the angle bisector.

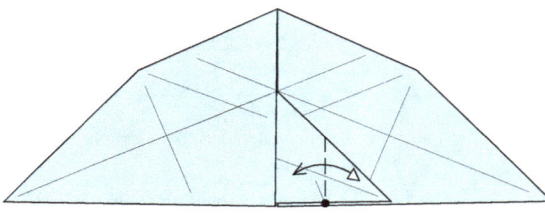

26. Precrease starting from the dotted intersection.

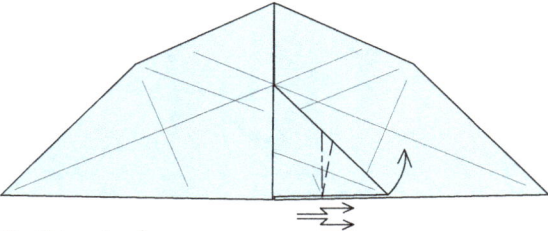

27. Crimp the flap up.

dolphin

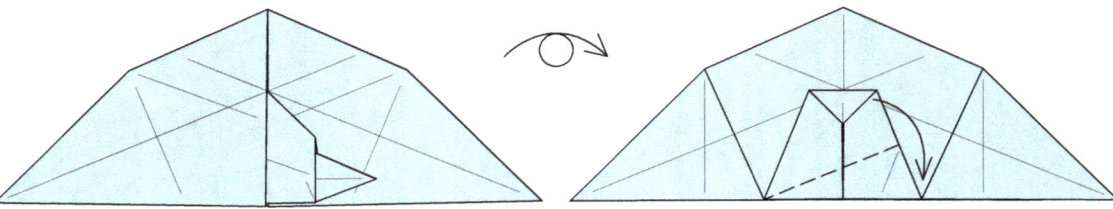

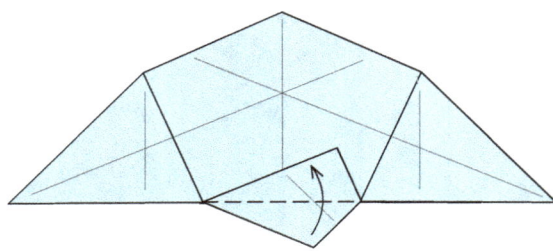

28. Turn over.

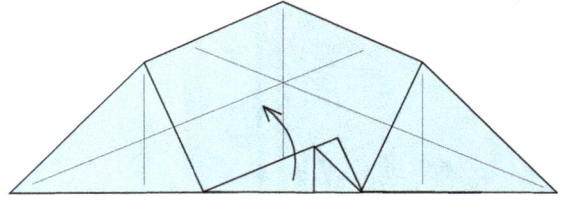

29. Valley fold so the top corner hits the bottom edge.

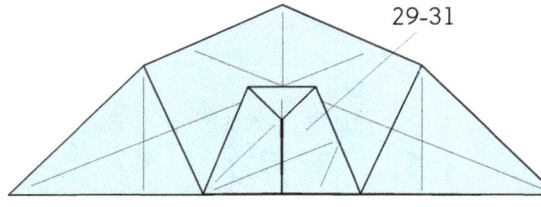

30. Valley fold the flap up.

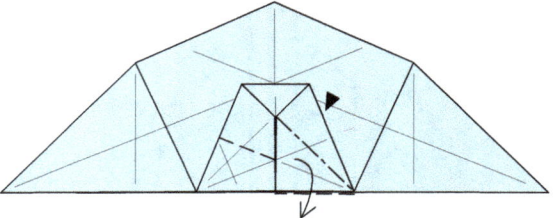

31. Unfold the pleat.

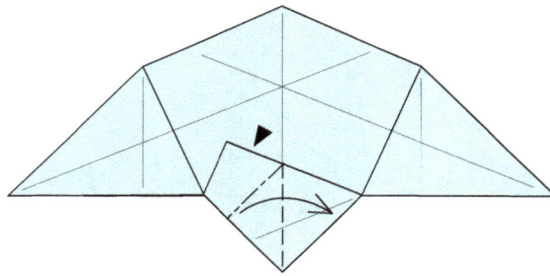

32. Repeat steps 29-31 in mirror image.

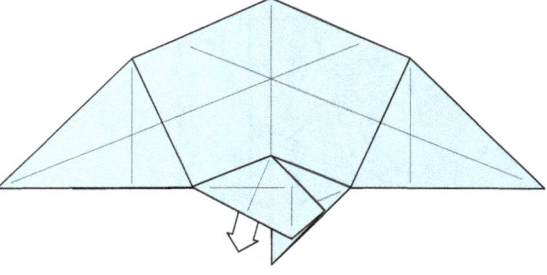

33. Squash fold the flap using the existing creases.

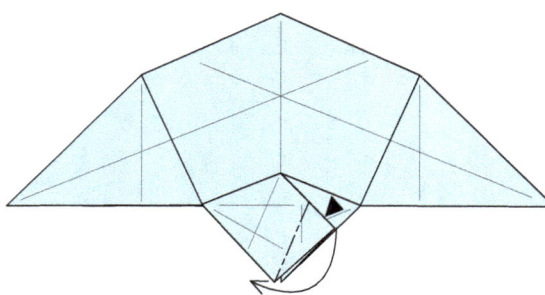

34. Squash fold the flap over.

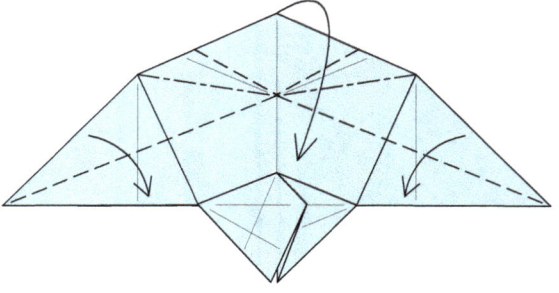

35. Pull out the trapped layer and flatten.

36. Reverse fold along the angle bisector.

37. Squash fold the top down. The bottom folds are along the angle bisectors and the mountain folds extend to the corners. The top folds should form naturally.

dolphin

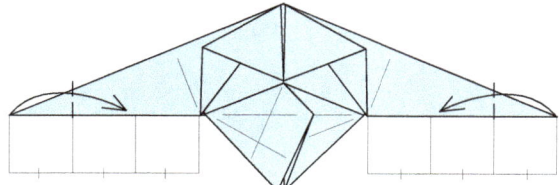

38. Valley fold the corners in along the indicated 1/3rd divisions.

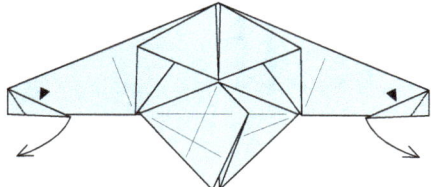

39. Squash fold the flaps down.

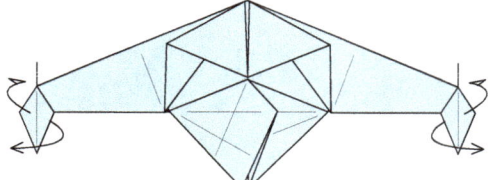

40. Flip the flaps behind.

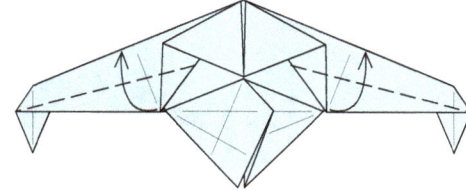

41. Starting from the outside corners, valley fold the top layers up to the top edge.

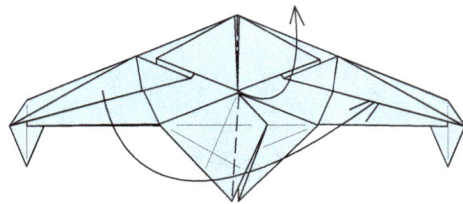

42. Valley fold in half while pulling up the top flap and squash folding it flat. Also, tuck one flap into the pocket at the opposite side.

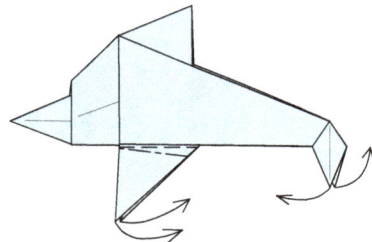

43. Pleat the bottom flaps up. Spread apart the tail flaps. Flatten the connecting ridge on the underside of the tail flaps to form a stronger lock.

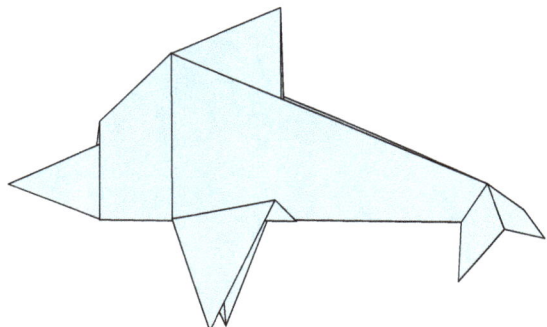

44. Completed *Dolphin*.

Snail

snail

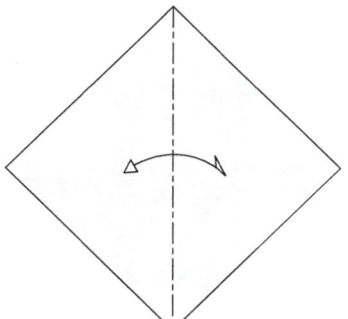

1. Precrease in half along the diagonal with a mountain fold.

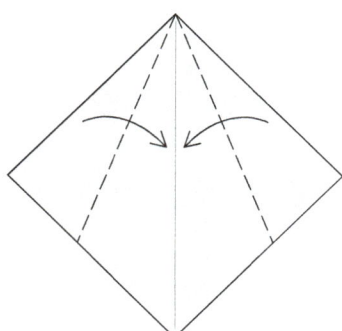

2. Valley fold the sides to the center.

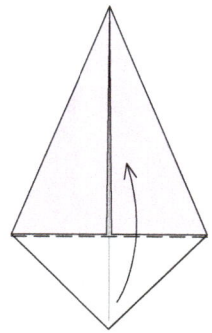

3. Valley fold the corner up.

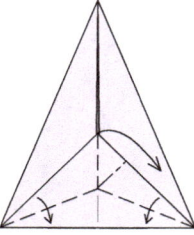

4. Rabbit ear the flap.

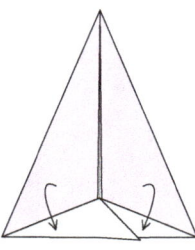

5. Bring the single layers around to the surface.

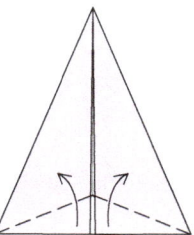

6. Valley fold up, to align with the edges below.

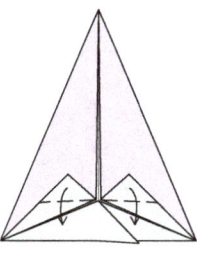

7. Valley fold the corners down, so the top edges are straight.

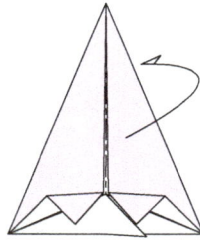

8. Mountain fold in half.

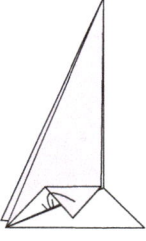

9. Tuck the corner into the pocket.

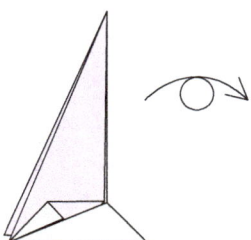

10. Turn over.

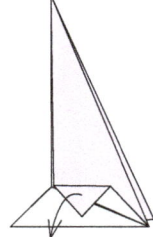

11. Unfold the pleat.

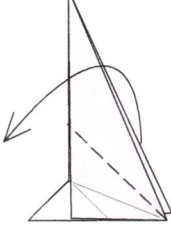

12. Valley fold the long flap over.

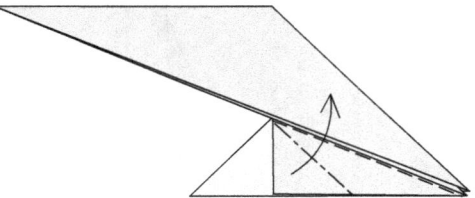
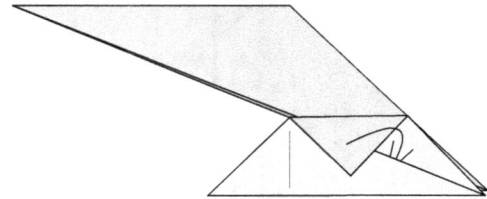

13. Reform the pleat.

14. Tuck the corner into the pocket.

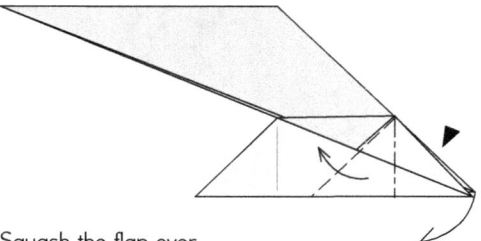
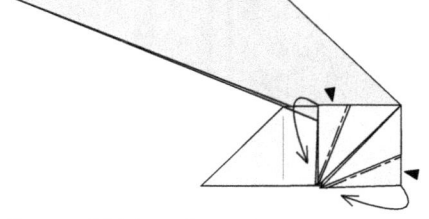

15. Squash the flap over.

16. Reverse fold the sides.

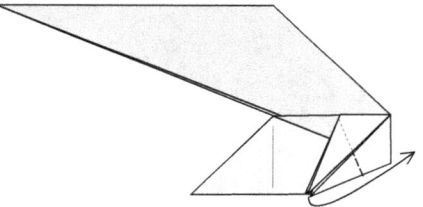
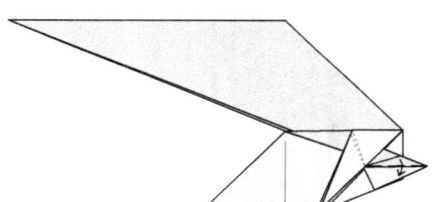

17. Valley fold the trapped flap over, not quite starting from the corner.

18. Swivel the colored layer over.

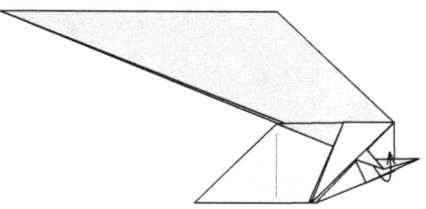
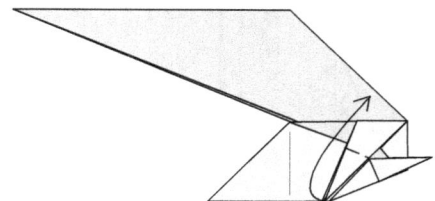

19. Wrap the single layer around.

20. Valley fold the flap up.

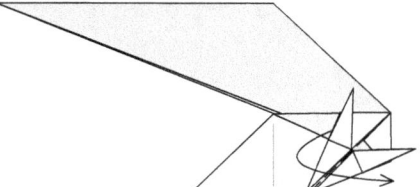

21. Valley fold over.

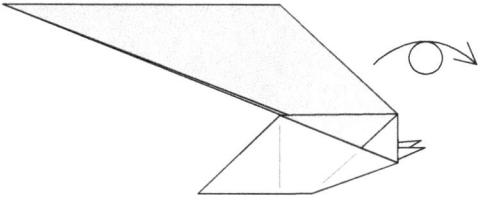

22. Turn over.

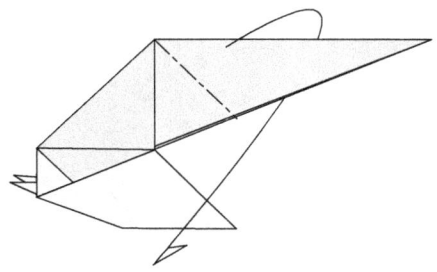

23. Mountain fold, pulling the tip of the flap through to lie on the surface of the model.

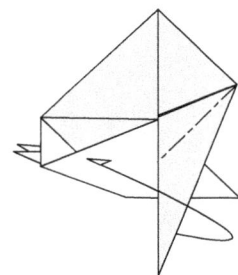

24. Mountain fold again, in a similar fashion as with the previous step.

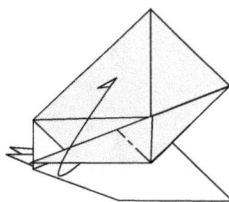

25. Form another mountain fold.

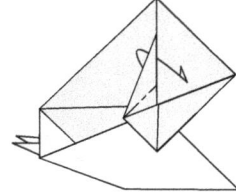

26. Mountain fold again.

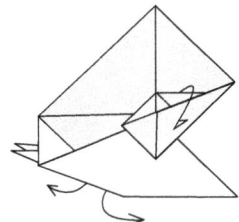

27. Mountain fold and open out the bottom.

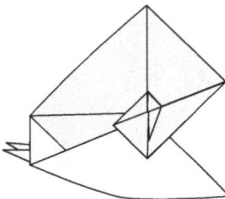

28. Completed *Snail*.

Shark

shark

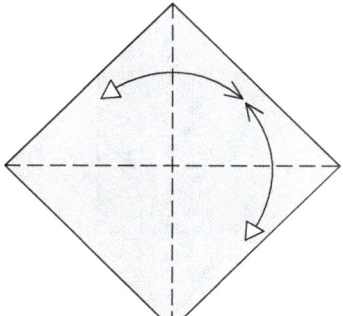

1. Precrease in half along the diagonals.

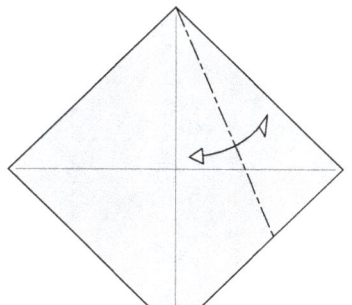

2. Precrease along the angle bisector with a mountain fold.

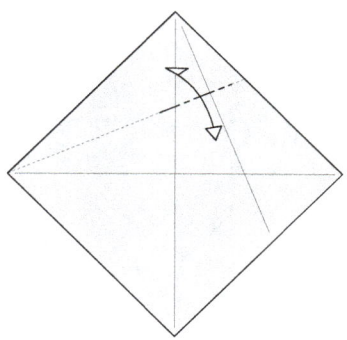

3. Precrease along the angle bisector with a mountain fold, creasing only at the indicated intersection.

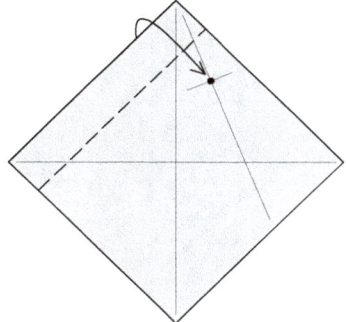

4. Valley fold, allowing the edge to hit the dotted intersection.

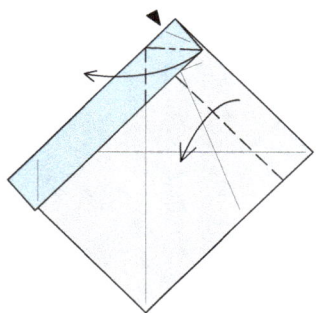

5. Valley fold the other side over to match, squash folding the top corner over.

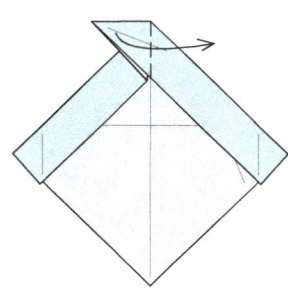

6. Swing over the center flap.

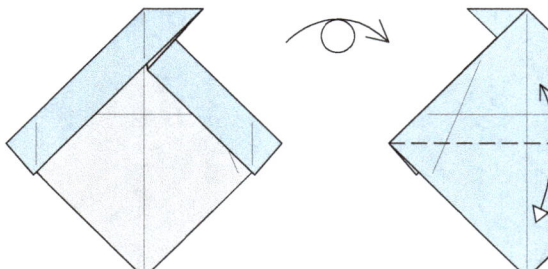

7. Turn over.

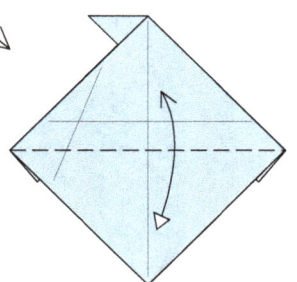

8. Precrease the top layer.

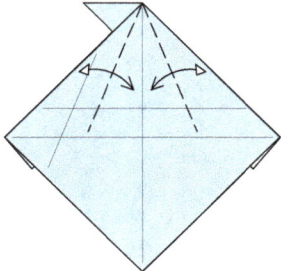

9. Precrease along the angle bisectors.

shark

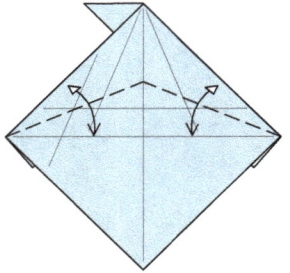
10. Precrease along the angle bisectors.

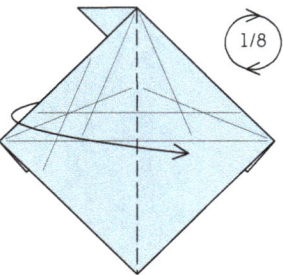
11. Valley fold in half. Rotate the model.

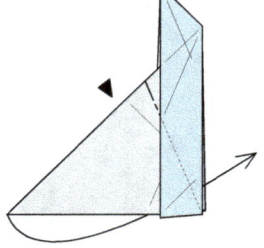
12. Reverse fold the center flap.

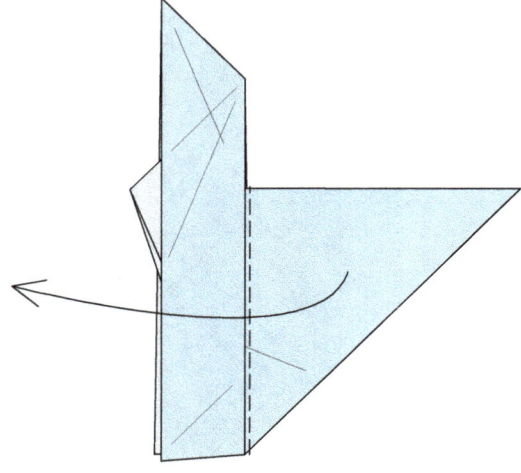
13. Valley fold the flap over.

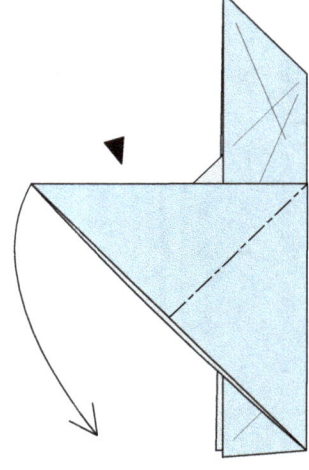
14. Squash fold the flap down.

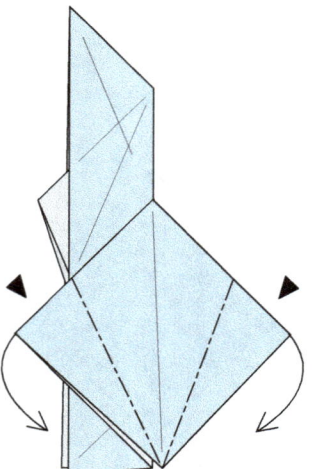
15. Reverse fold the sides.

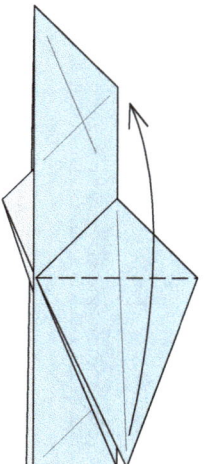
16. Valley fold up.

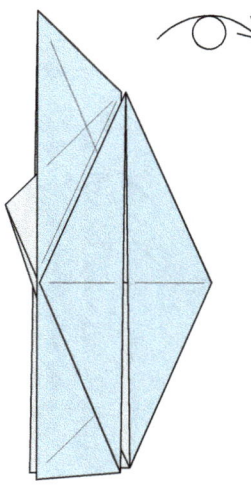
17. Turn over.

shark

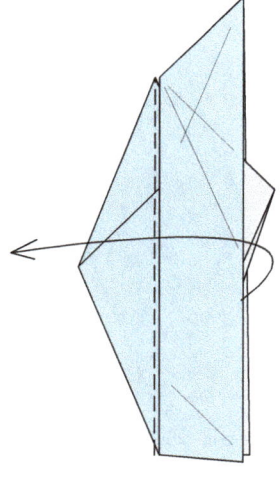

18. Open out the flap. The top will not lie flat.

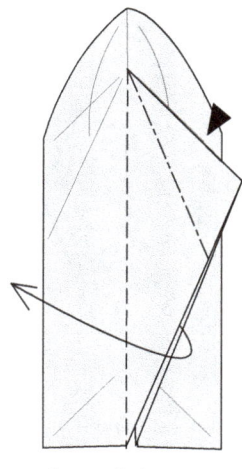

19. Spread squash the center.

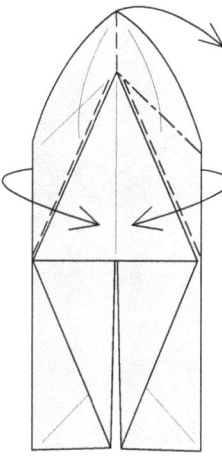

20. Rabbit ear the flap so it lies flat.

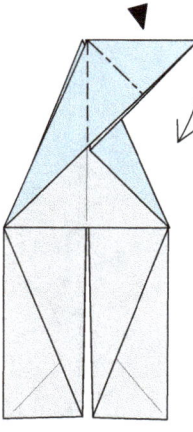

21. Squash fold the flap down.

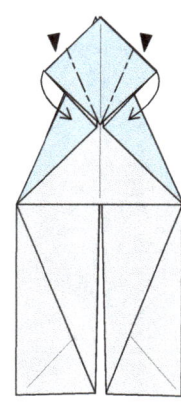

22. Reverse fold the sides.

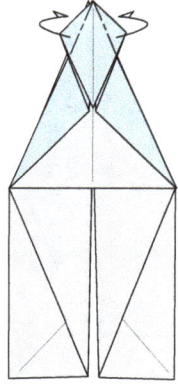

23. Mountain fold the corners inside.

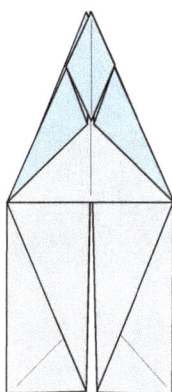

24. Turn over.

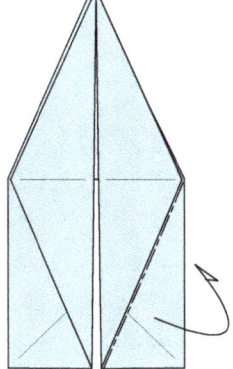

25. Mountain fold the edge behind.

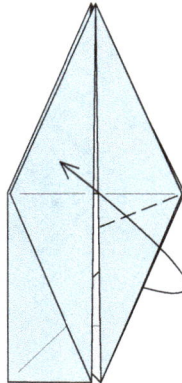

26. Valley fold up so that the hidden edge lies straight.

shark

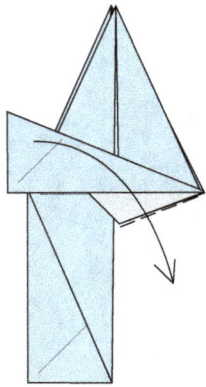

27. Swing back down.

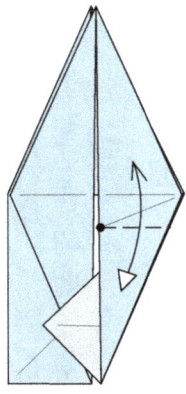

28. Precrease starting from the dotted intersection.

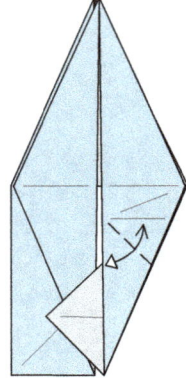

29. Precrease along the angle bisector.

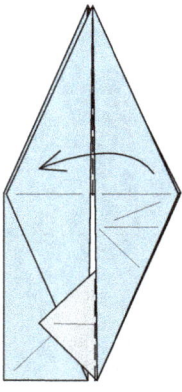

30. Swing over one flap.

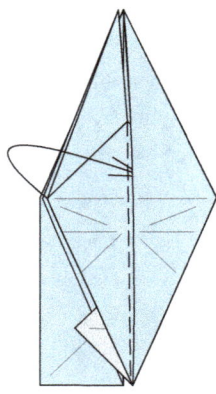

31. Tuck the flap into the pocket.

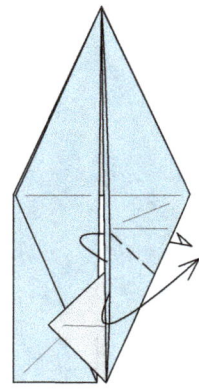

32. Outside reverse fold along the existing crease.

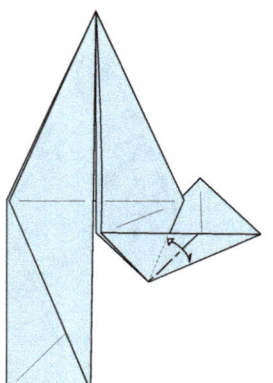

33. Precrease along the angle bisector with a mountain fold.

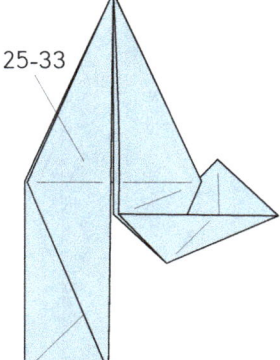

34. Repeat steps 25-33 in mirror image.

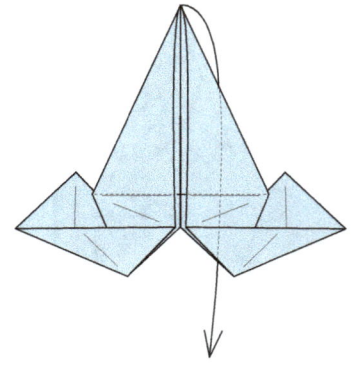

35. Swing down the hidden flap.

shark

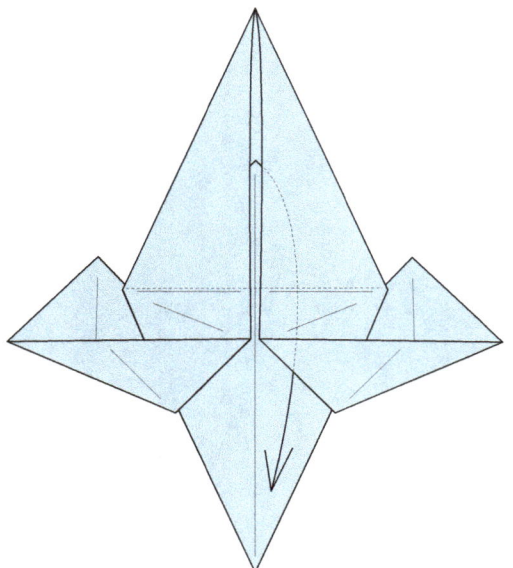

36. Swing down the smaller hidden flap.

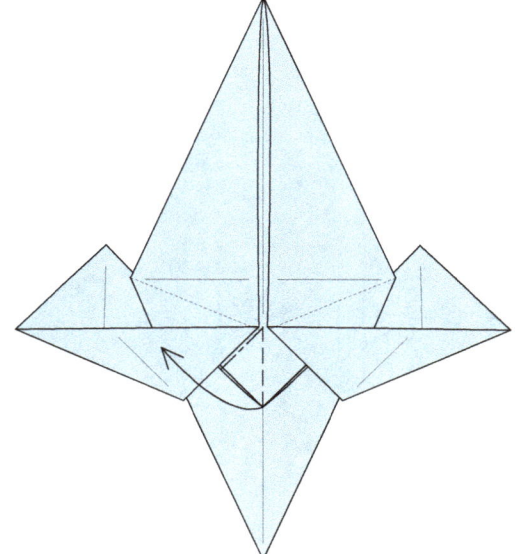

37. Rabbit ear the flap.

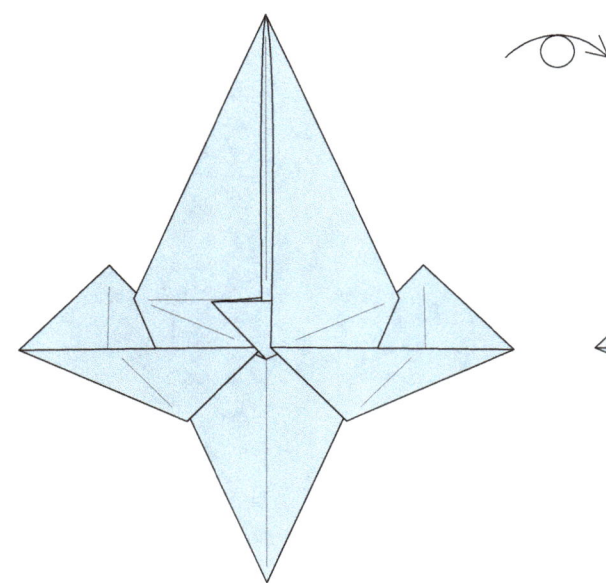

38. Turn over.

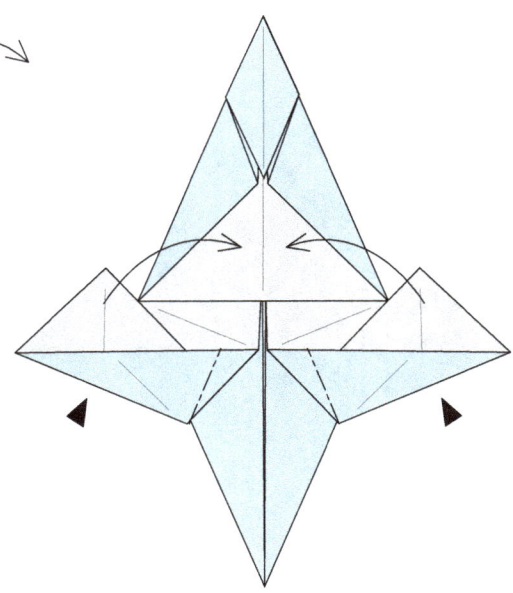

39. Squash fold the sides inwards using the existing creases.

shark

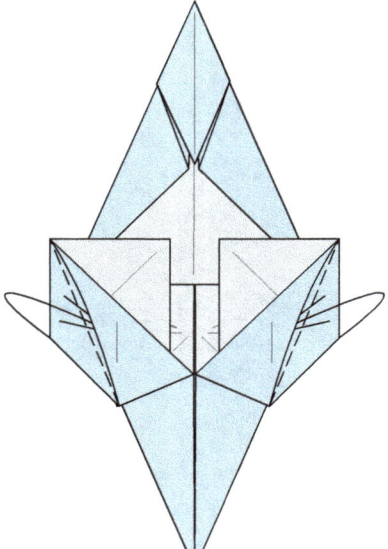 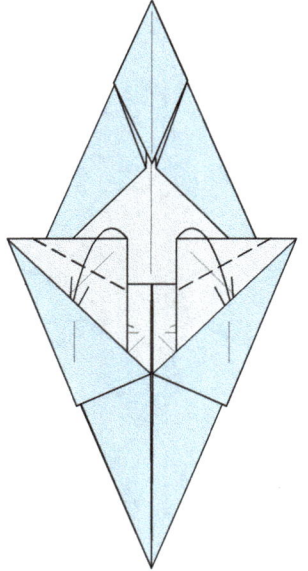 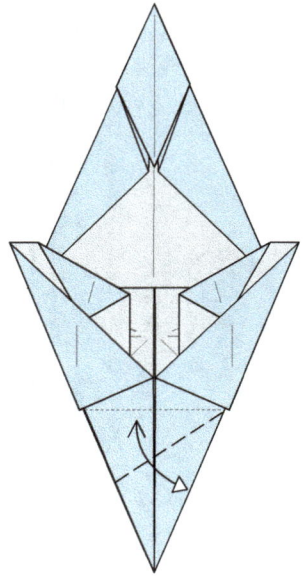

40. Tuck the flaps into the pockets.

41. Valley fold so the tips are tucked under the edges.

42. Lightly precrease along the angle bisector.

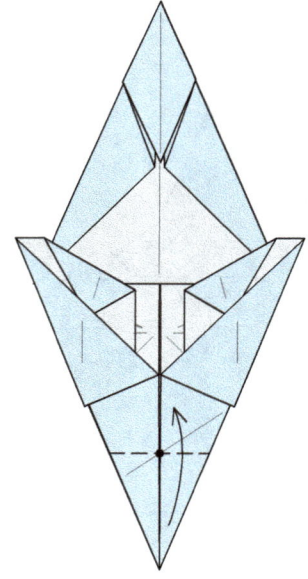 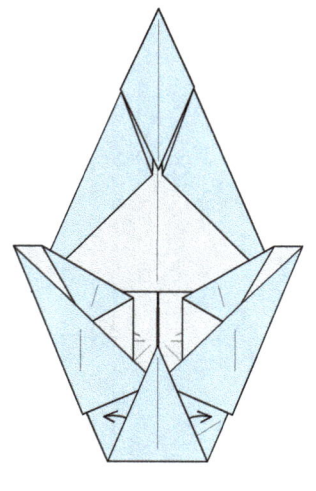 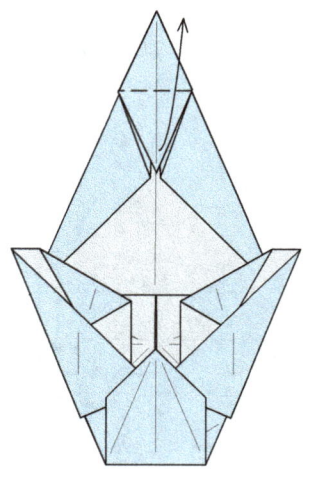

43. Valley fold through the dotted intersection.

44. Slide the sides out.

45. Valley fold the flap up.

shark

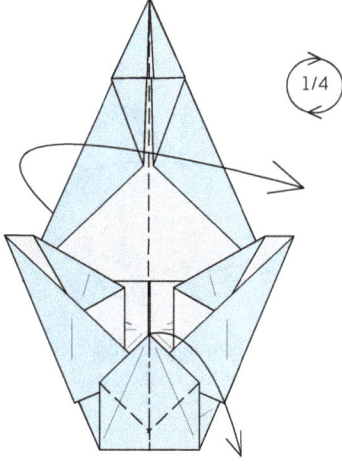

46. Valley fold in half while reverse folding the bottom corner. Rotate the model.

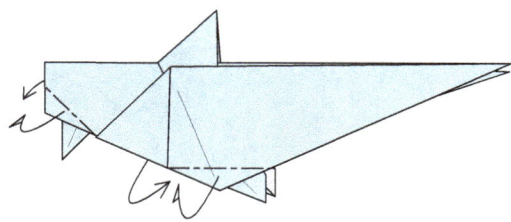

47. Mountain fold the indicated corners in on both sides.

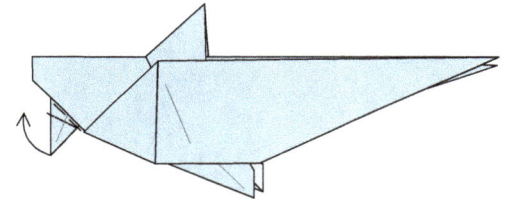

48. Pleat the flap inside.

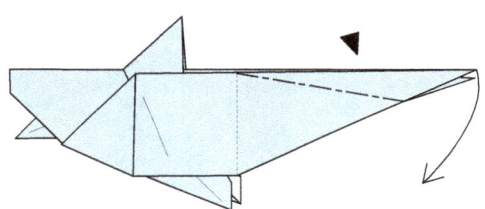

49. Reverse fold the flap down.

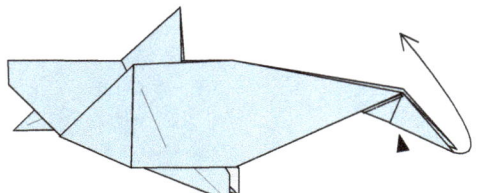

50. Reverse fold the flap up.

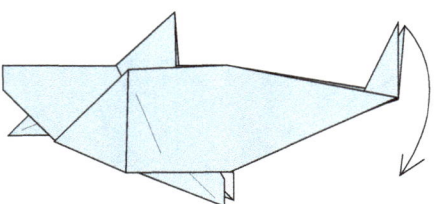

51. Pull the trapped flap down.

shark

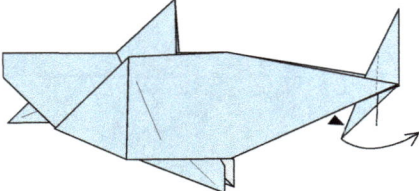

52. Reverse fold the flap outwards.

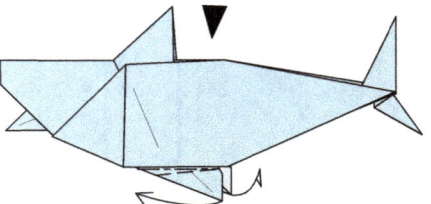

53. Pleat the side flaps up. Round out the body.

54. Completed *Shark*.

Walrus

walrus

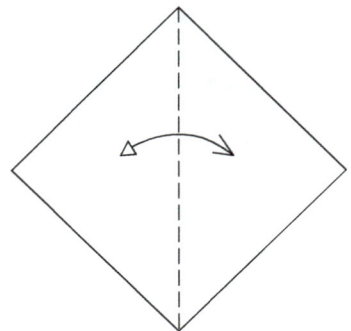

1. Precrease along the diagonal.

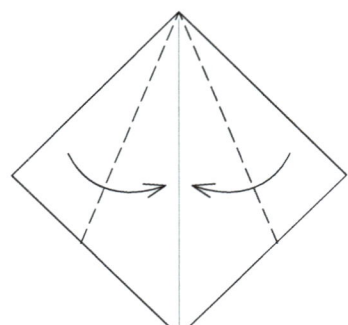

2. Valley fold to the center.

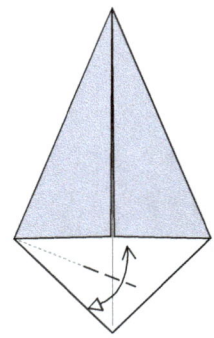

3. Precrease the middle along the angle bisector.

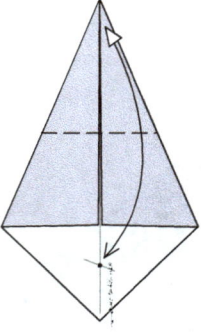

4. Precrease to the dotted intersection of creases.

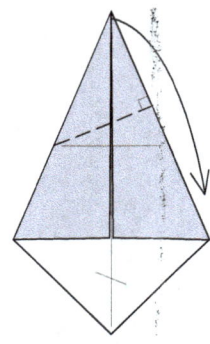

5. Valley fold down, keeping the side edges aligned.

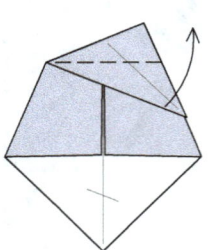

6. Valley fold the flap up.

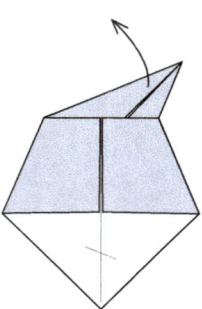

7. Unfold the pleat.

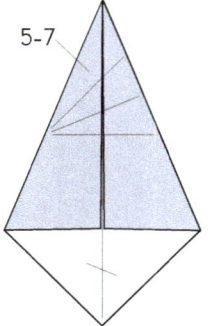

8. Repeat steps 5-7 in mirror image.

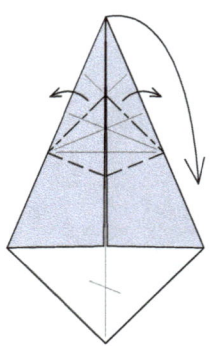

9. Spread open the sides and squash fold the flap down.

60

walrus

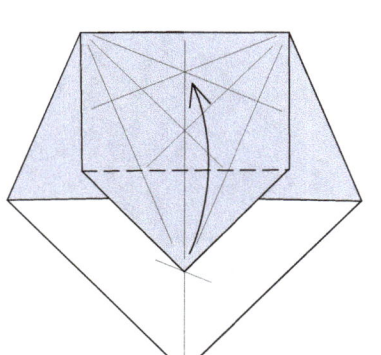

10. Valley fold the corner up.

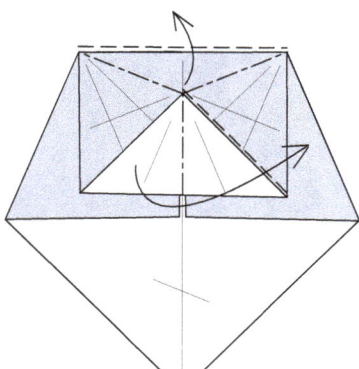

11. Rabbit ear the top layer, allowing it to collapse upwards.

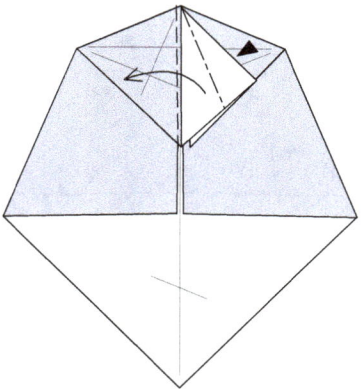

12. Squash fold the center flap.

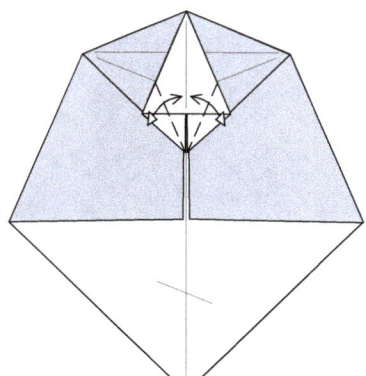

13. Precrease along the angle bisectors.

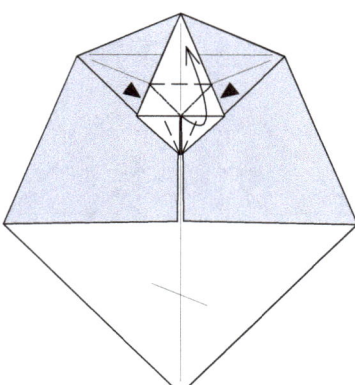

14. Pull the edge up while squash folding the sides.

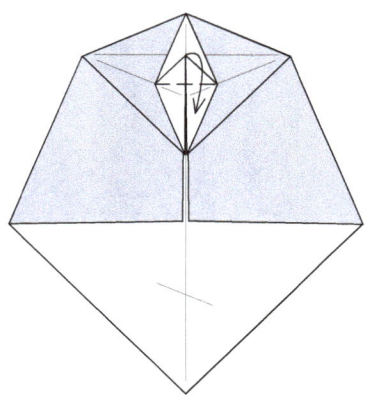

15. Valley fold the corner down.

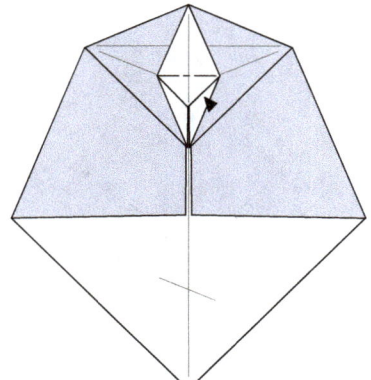

16. Reverse fold the corner inside.

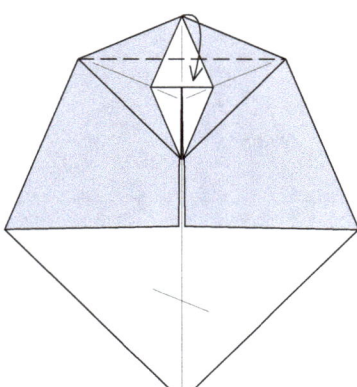

17. Valley fold the top edge down.

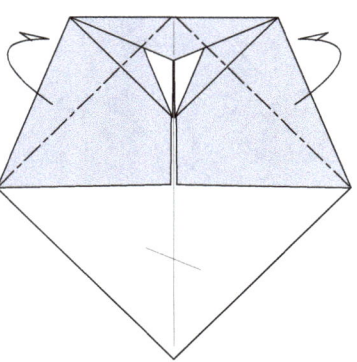

18. Mountain fold the edges behind.

walrus

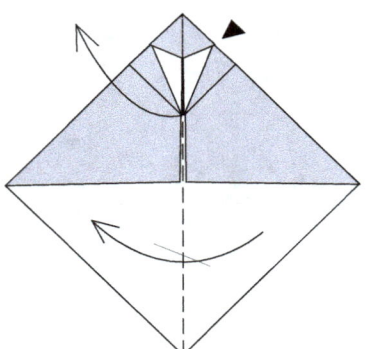

19. Valley fold in half while squash folding the top corner.

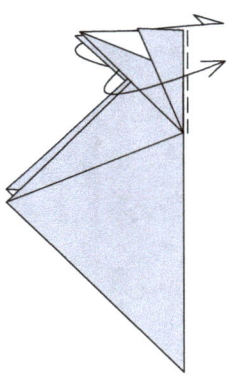

20. Outside reverse fold the cluster of flaps.

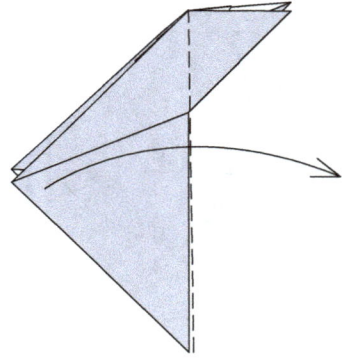

21. Open out the model along the center.

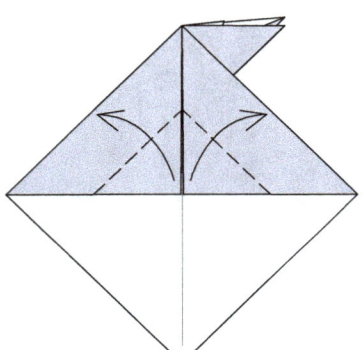

22. Valley fold the corners outwards.

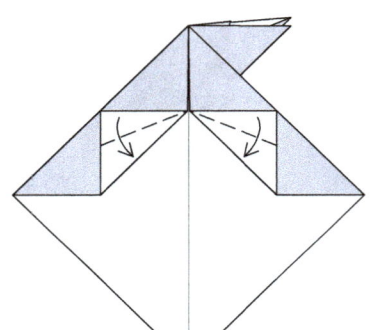

23. Valley fold along the angle bisectors.

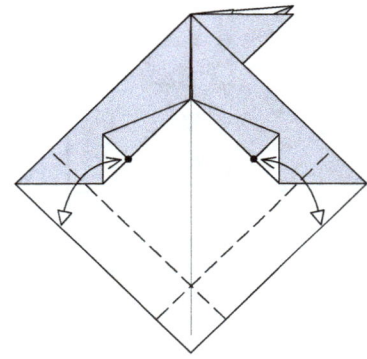

24. Precrease towards the dotted corners.

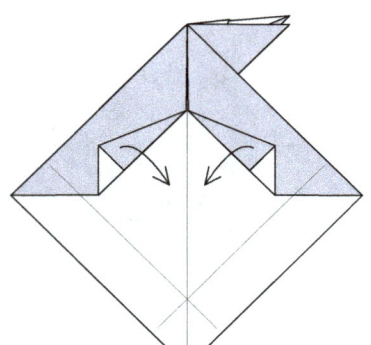

25. Unfold the pleats.

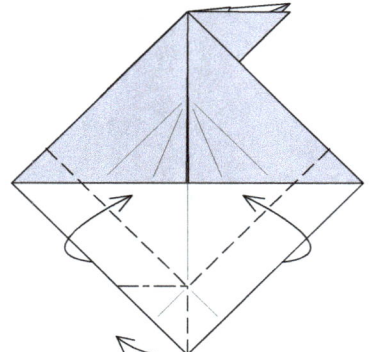

26. Rabbit ear along the existing creases.

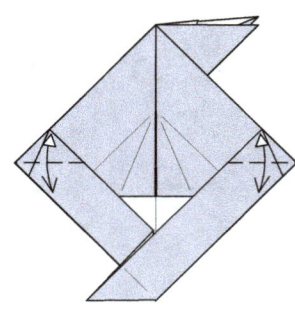

27. Precrease the top layers.

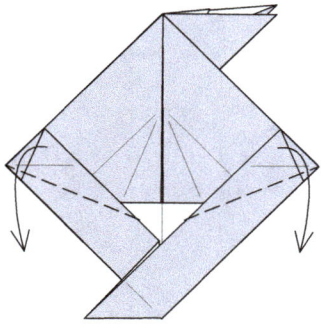 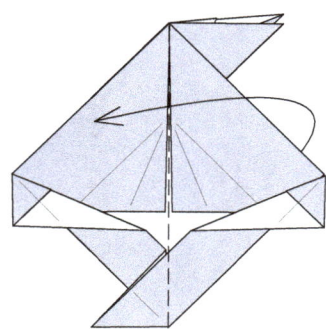 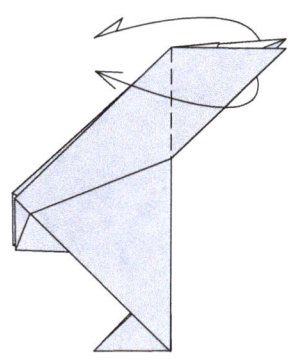

28. Valley fold the flaps down so the creases meet the outer edges.

29. Valley fold in half.

30. Outside reverse fold the cluster of flaps.

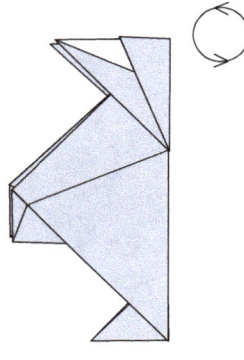 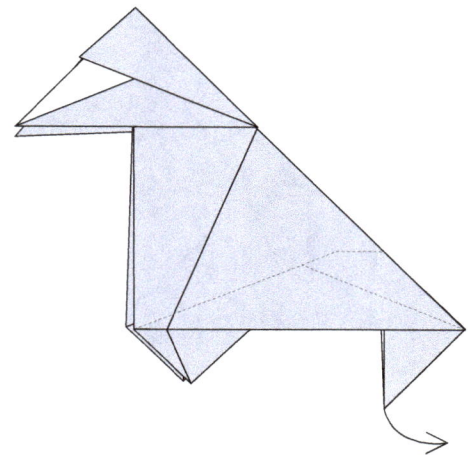

31. Rotate the model.

32. Slide the bottom flap down until it lies straight. Hidden folds will form to accomplish this.

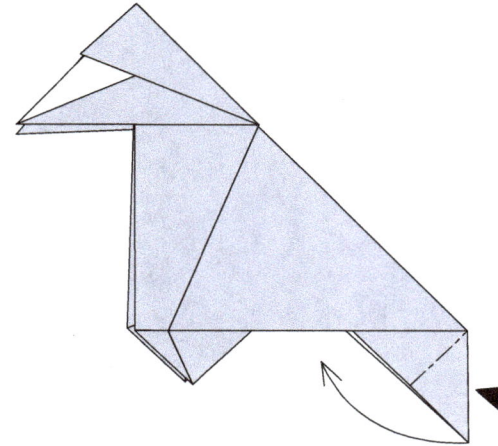 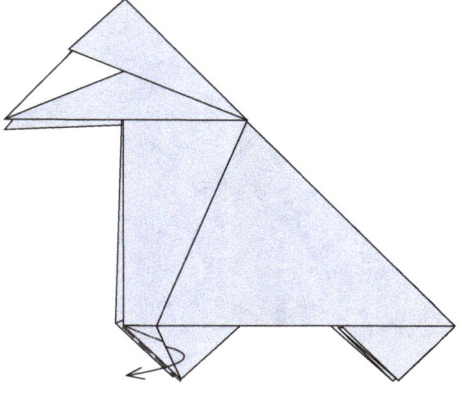

33. Reverse fold the corner up.

34. Slide out the top edge and flatten.

63

walrus

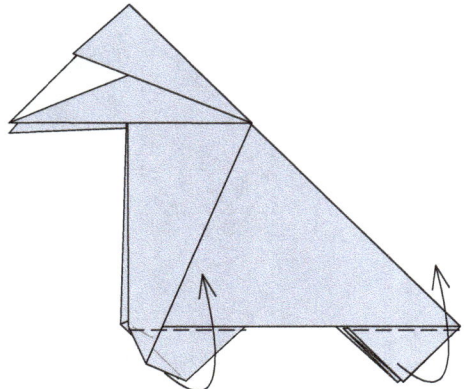

35. Valley fold the flaps up.

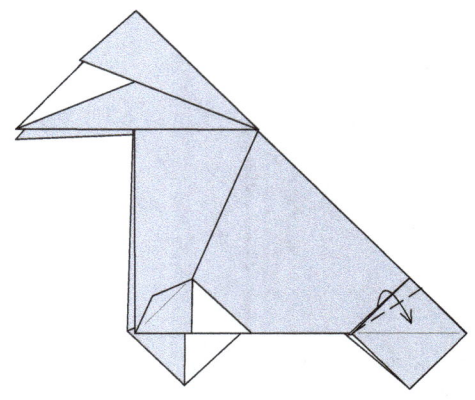

36. Valley fold the edge of the flap slightly.

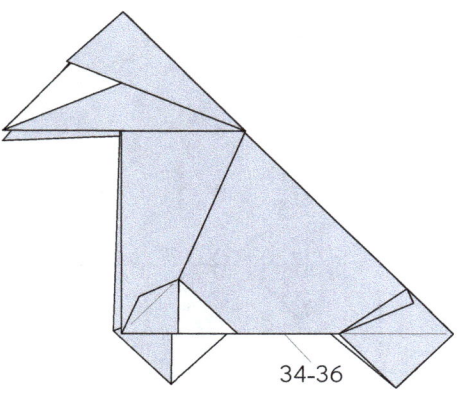

37. Repeat steps 34-36 behind.

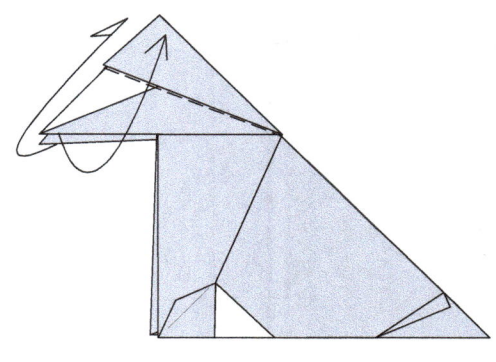

38. Valley fold the outer flaps up.

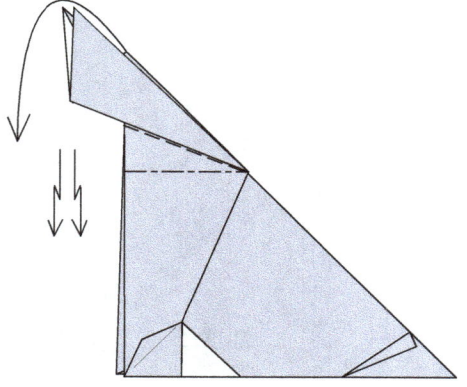

39. Crimp the top section down, so that the top edges lie straight.

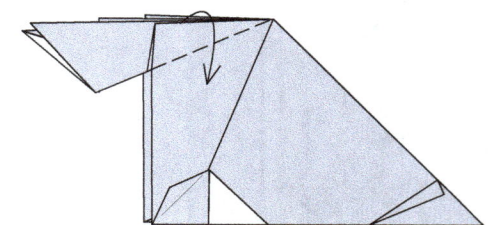

40. Lightly swing the top edge down.

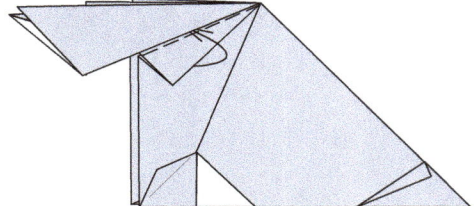

41. Tuck the flap into the pocket.

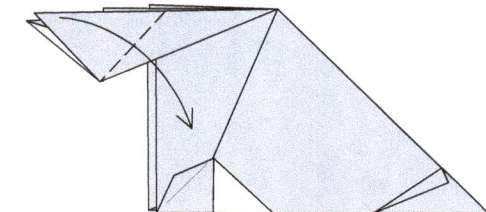

42. Valley fold the flap over.

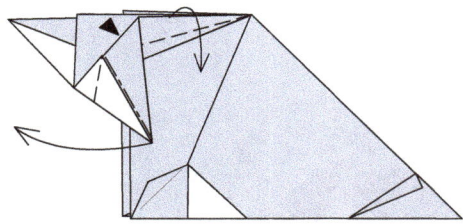

43. Squash fold the flap over.

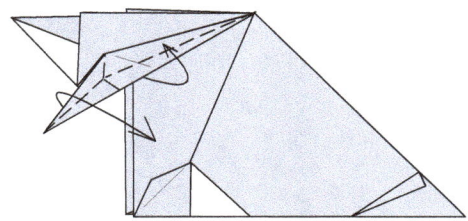

44. Swing the flap back while incorporating a reverse fold.

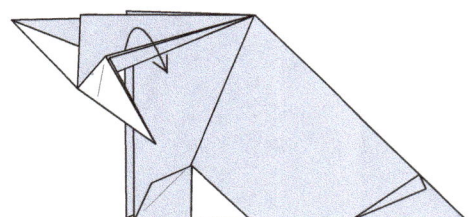

45. Tuck the edges into the pocket.

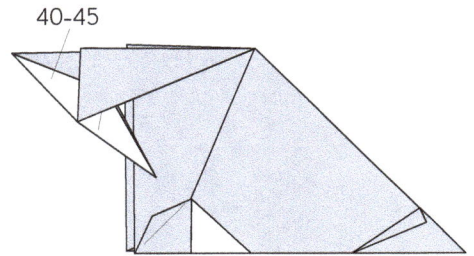

46. Repeat steps 40-45 behind.

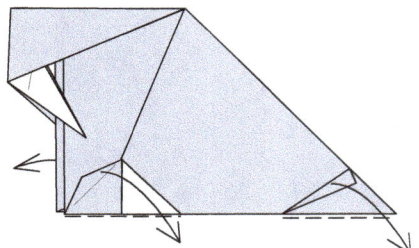

47. Swing the side flaps down and spread apart the body slightly.

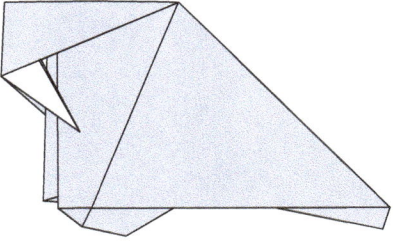

48. Completed *Walrus*.

Pelican

pelican

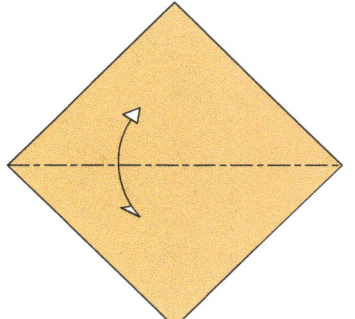

1. Precrease the diagonal with a mountain fold.

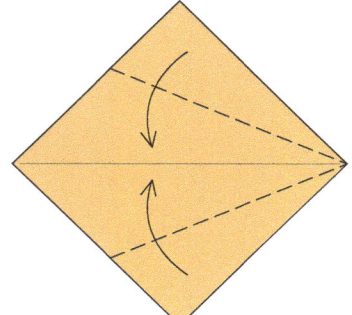

2. Valley fold the sides to the center.

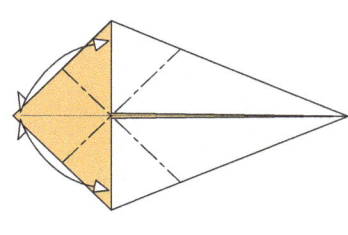

3. Precrease the side edges in half with mountain folds.

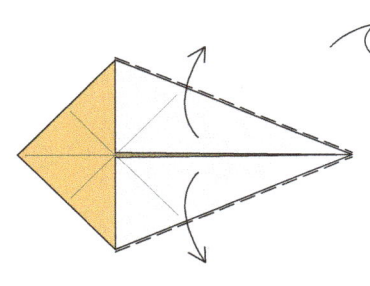

4. Open out the sides. Turn over.

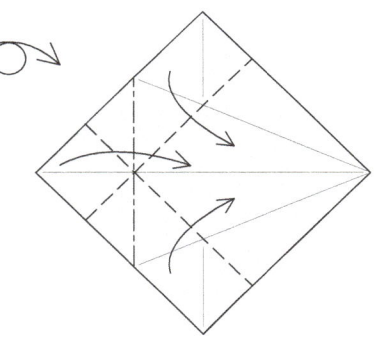

5. Extend the existing creases and collapse the side corner over.

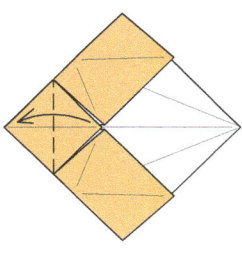

6. Valley fold the corner over.

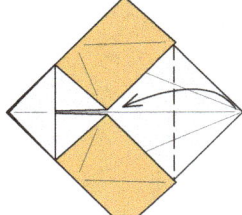

7. Valley fold to the intersection of creases.

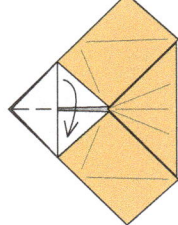

8. Swing one flap down.

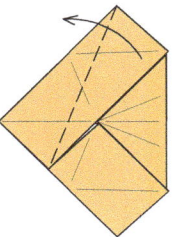

9. Valley fold from corner to corner.

pelican

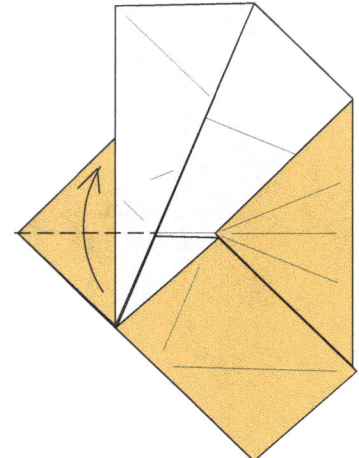

10. Swing the flap back up.

11. Repeat steps 8-10 on the bottom.

12. Rabbit ear the flap.

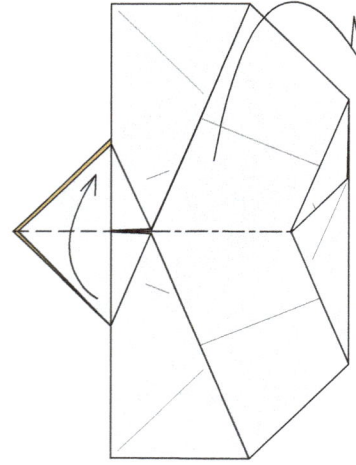

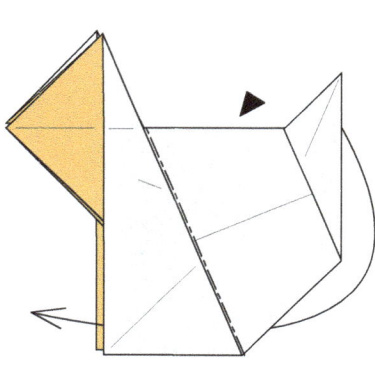

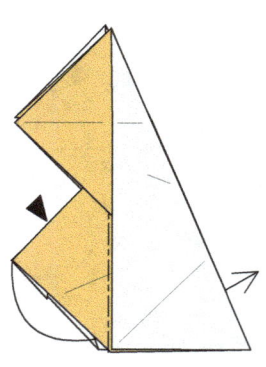

13. Mountain fold in half while swinging a flap up.

14. Reverse fold the flap through.

15. Reverse fold the flap, allowing the hidden corner to pop out.

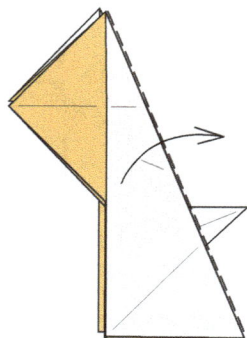

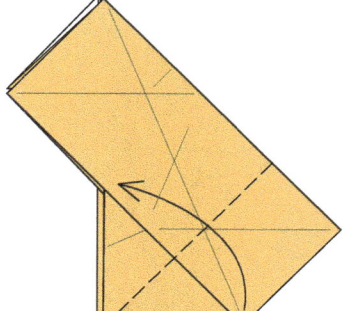

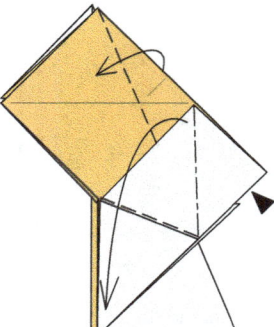

16. Open out the top layer.

17. Valley fold along the angle bisector.

18. Squash fold the corner down while valley folding the side edge.

pelican

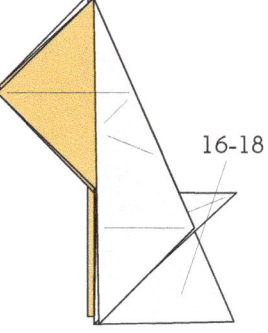 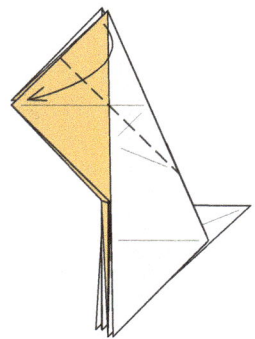 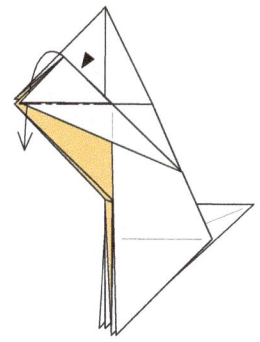

19. Repeat steps 16-18 behind.   20. Valley fold towards the corner.   21. Reverse fold the corner down.

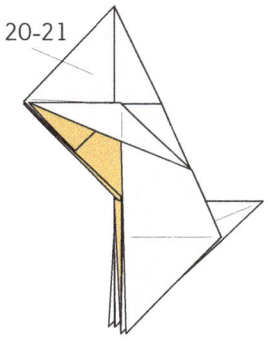 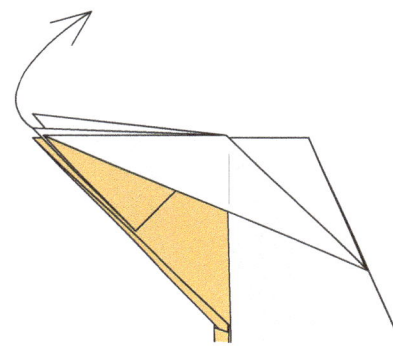

22. Repeat steps 20-21 behind.   23. Raise the center corner up, releasing the trapped layers.

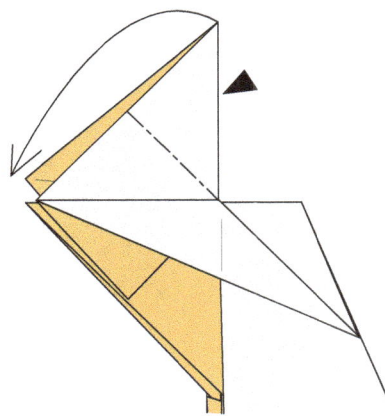 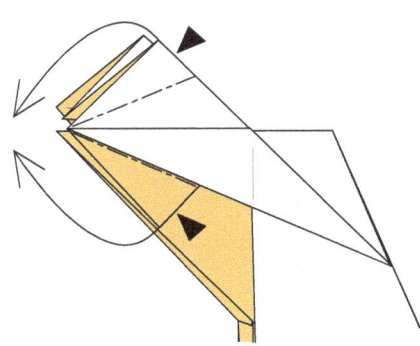

24. Reverse fold the corner down.   25. Reverse fold the corners.

69

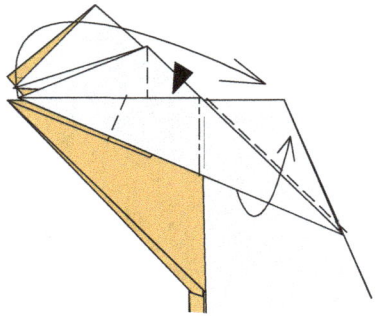

26. Swing the flap over while spreading apart the bottom section.

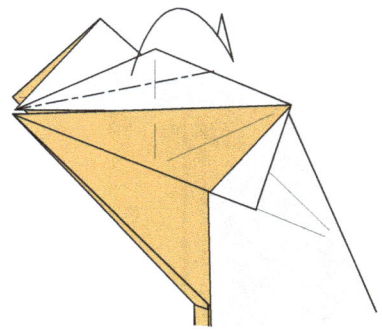

27. Mountain fold along the angle bisector.

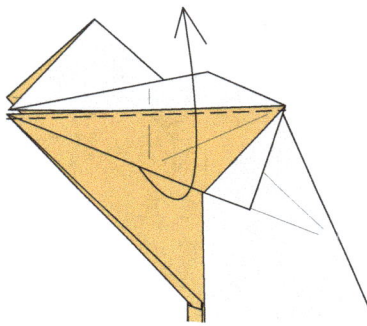

28. Swing the flap up.

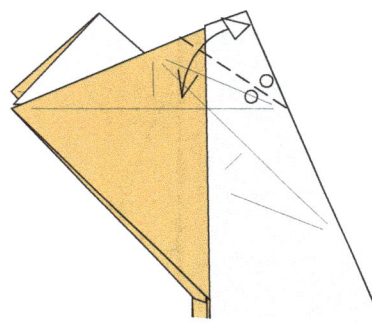

29. Precrease along the indicated angle bisector.

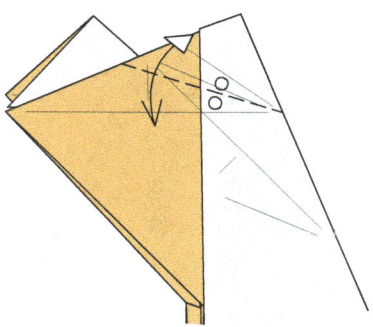

30. Precrease along the indicated angle bisector.

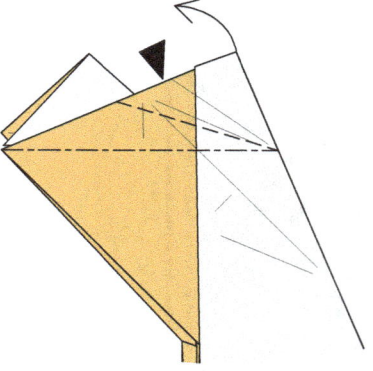

31. Reverse fold in and out along the existing creases.

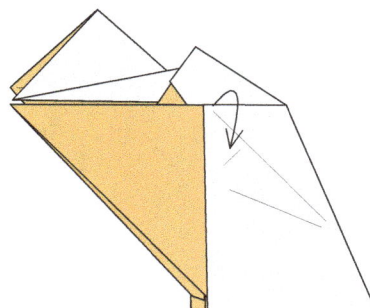

32. Pull out the trapped single layer.

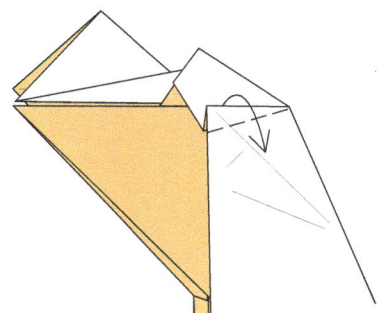

33. Valley fold the corner down.

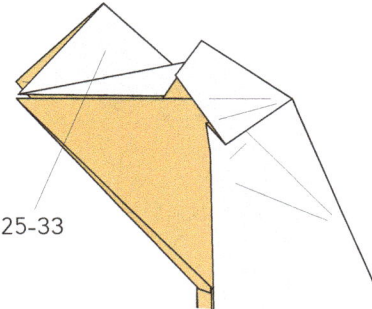

34. Repeat steps 25-33 behind.

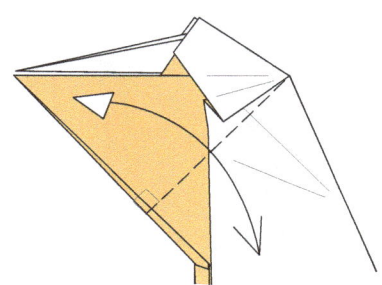

35. Precrease through all layers.

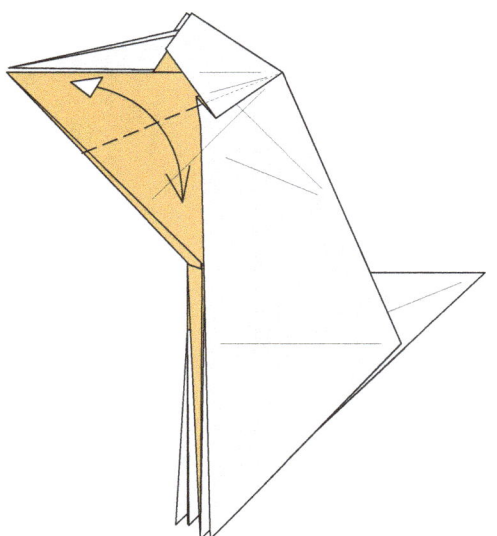

36. Precrease along the angle bisector.

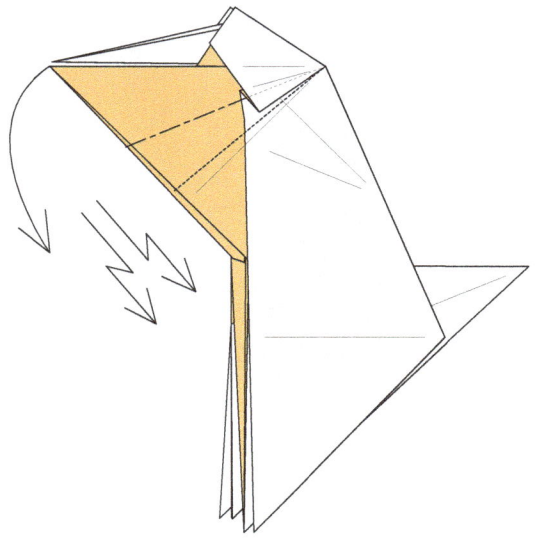

37. Crimp down so the top edge lies straight. The mountain fold is along the existing crease.

pelican

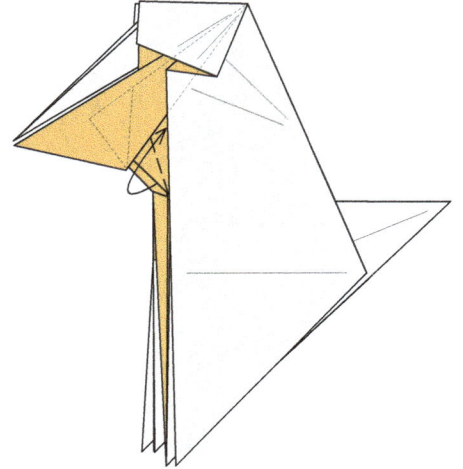

38. Swivel fold the edge in.

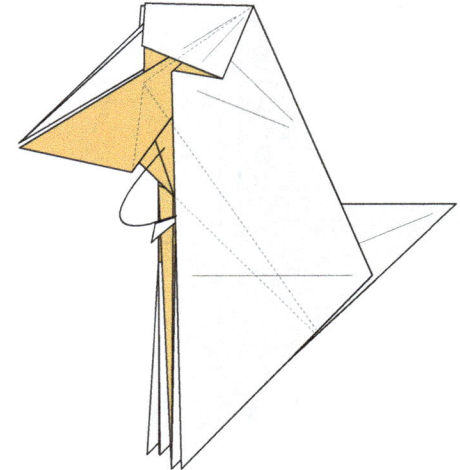

39. Mountain fold the hidden edge.

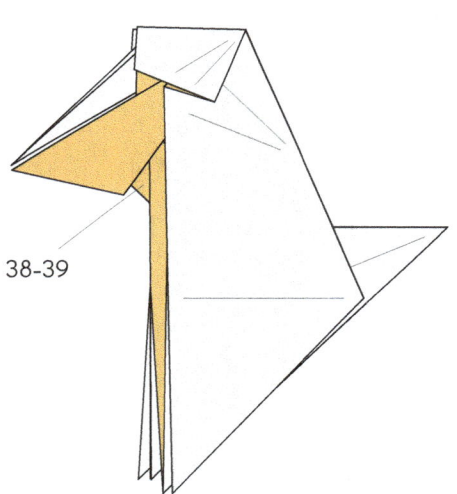

40. Repeat steps 38-39 behind.

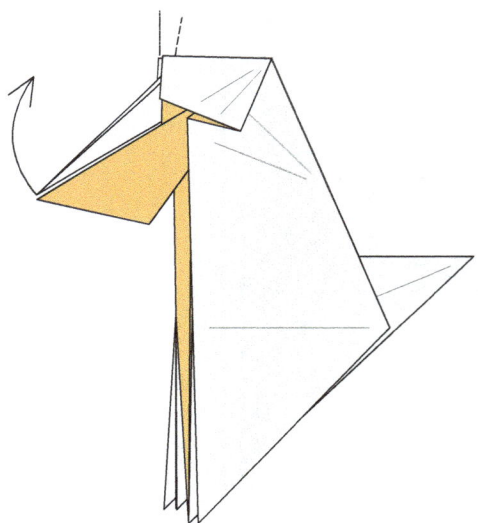

41. Crimp the flap up slightly.

pelican

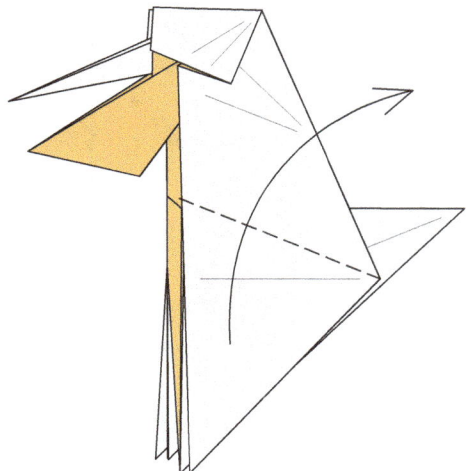

42. Swing the top flap up.

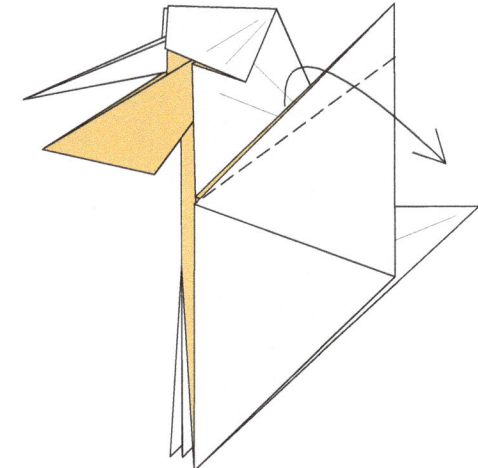

43. Valley fold part of the edge down.

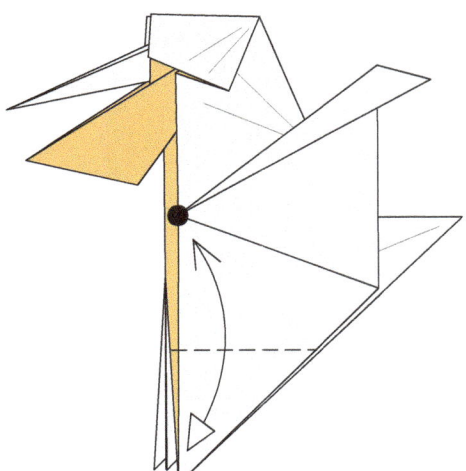

44. Precrease towards the dotted intersection.

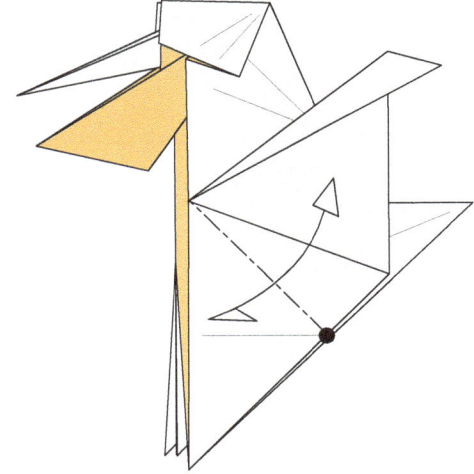

45. Precrease with a mountain fold using the dotted intersection.

pelican

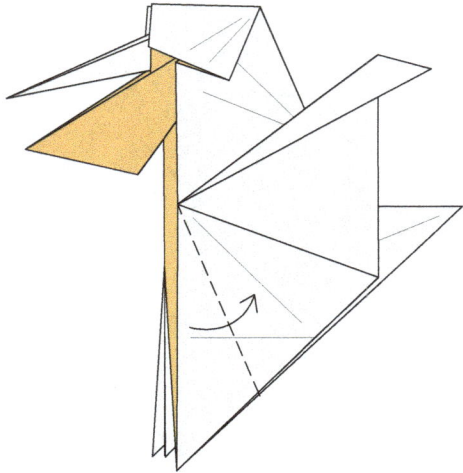

46. Valley fold towards the crease.

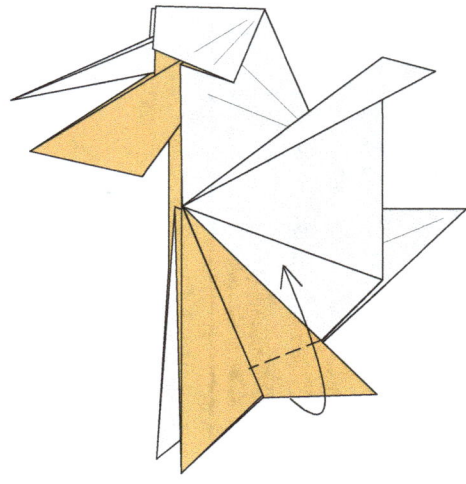

47. Valley fold the flap up so its side edge lies straight.

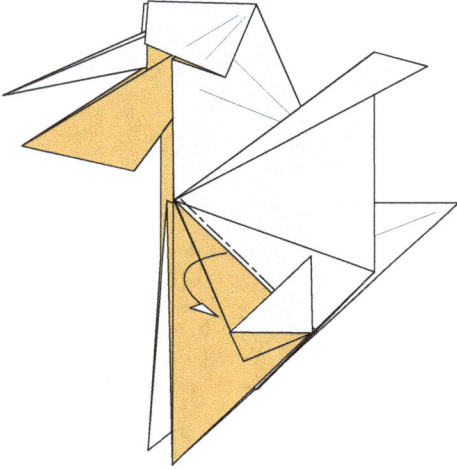

48. Mountain fold along the existing crease.

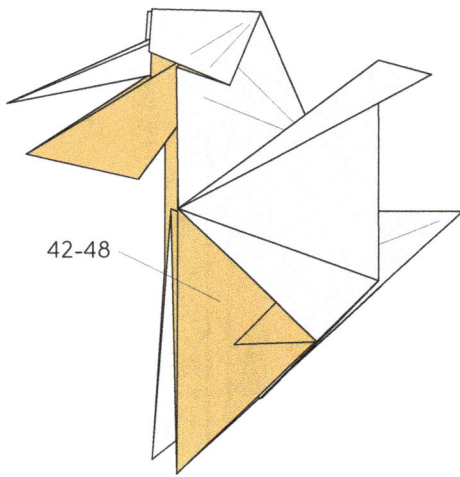

42–48

49. Repeat steps 42–48 behind.

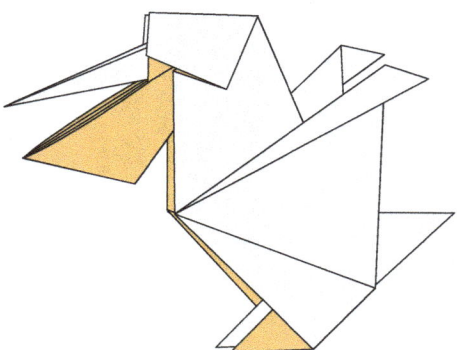

50. Completed *Pelican*.

Whale

whale

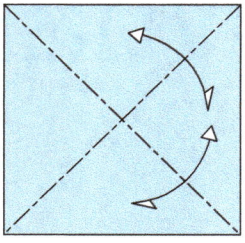

1. Precrease along the diagonals with mountain folds.

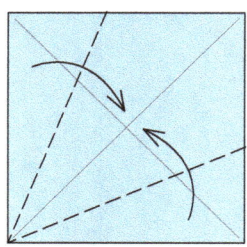

2. Valley fold to the center.

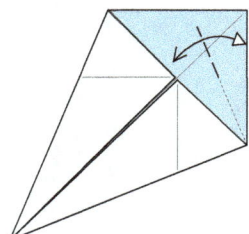

3. Precrease the middle along the angle bisector.

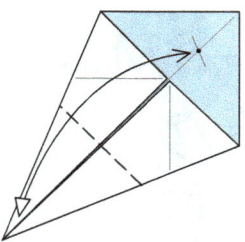

4. Precrease to the dotted intersection of creases.

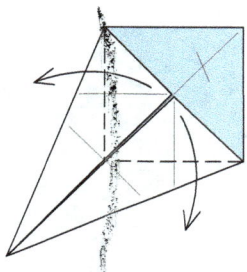

5. Valley fold the flaps outwards.

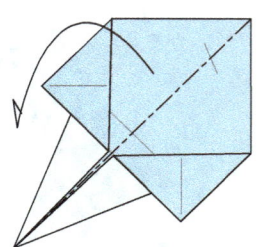

6. Mountain fold in half.

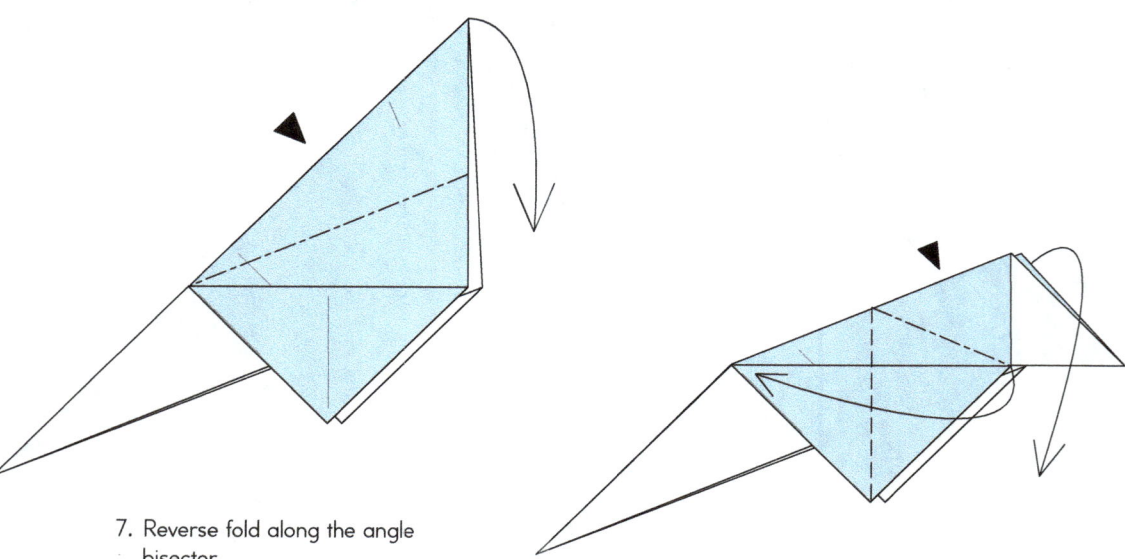

7. Reverse fold along the angle bisector.

8. Valley fold the top layer over, forming a squash fold.

whale

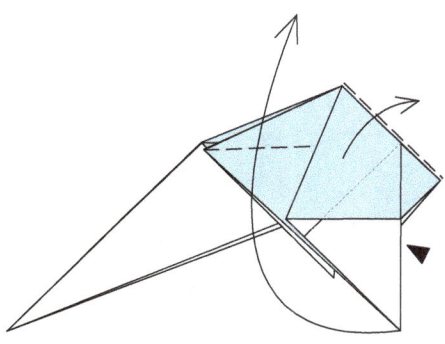

9. Squash fold the flap up.

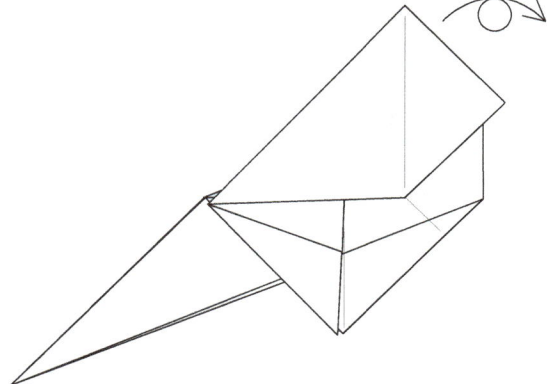

10. Turn over.

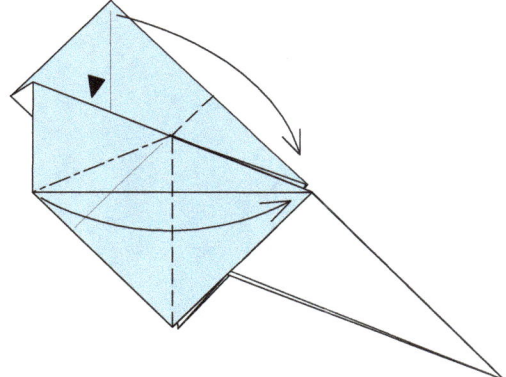

11. Valley fold the top layer over, forming a squash fold.

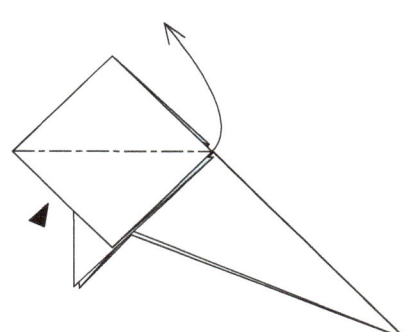

12. Raise the corner up, squash folding it flat.

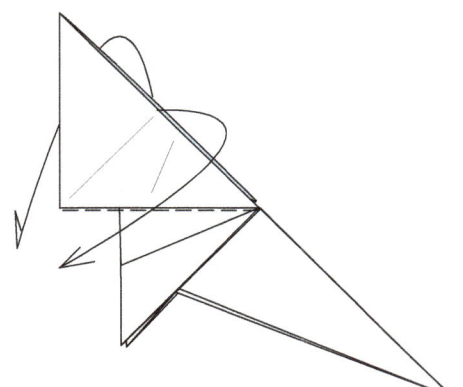

13. Wrap around the outer single layer.

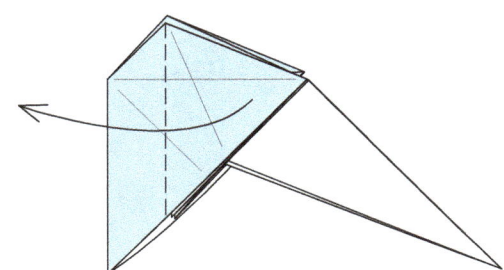

14. Valley fold the top flap over.

whale

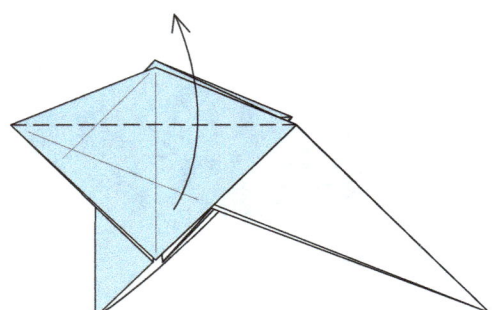

15. Valley fold the top layer up.

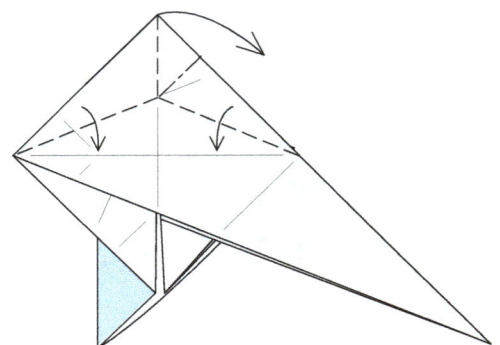

16. Rabbit ear the top corner.

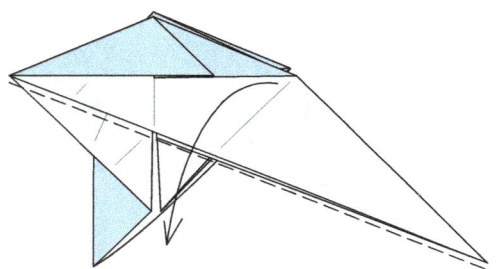

17. Swing the top section down.

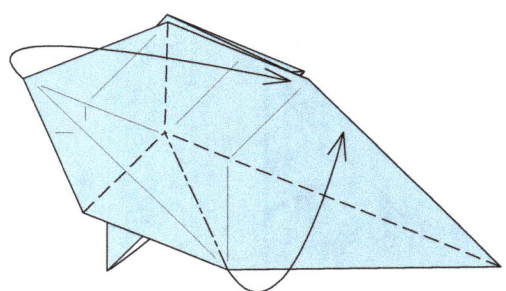

18. Swing the side over while incorporating a reverse fold.

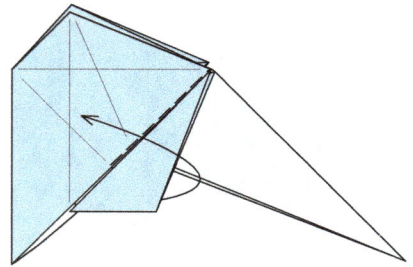

19. Valley fold the flap up.

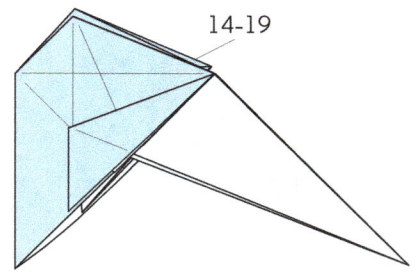

20. Repeat steps 14-19 behind.

whale

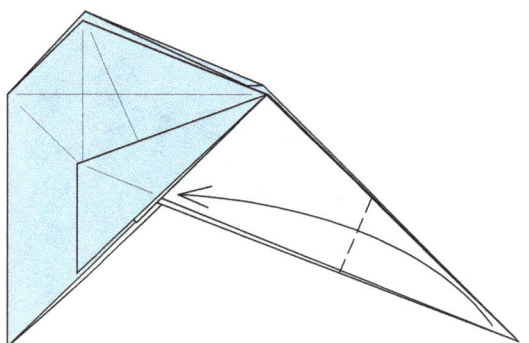

21. Valley fold the flap in half.

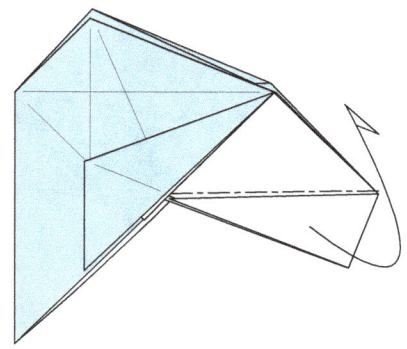

22. Mountain fold along the folded edge.

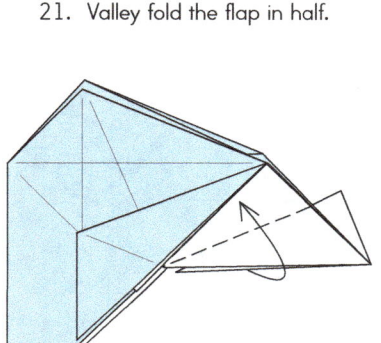

23. Valley fold along the angle bisector.

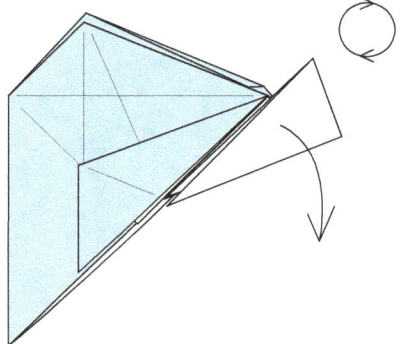

24. Unfold the pleat. Rotate the model slightly.

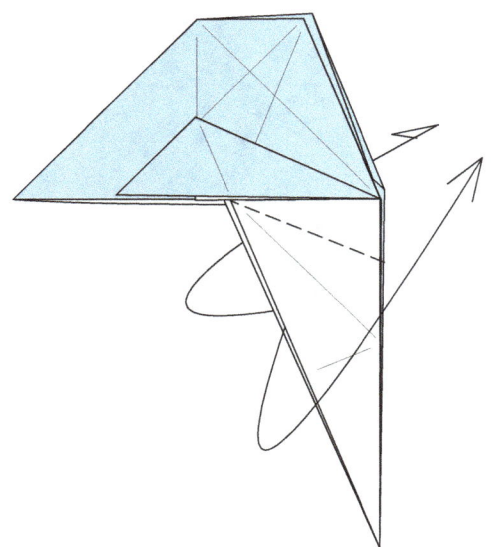

25. Outside reverse fold along the existing crease.

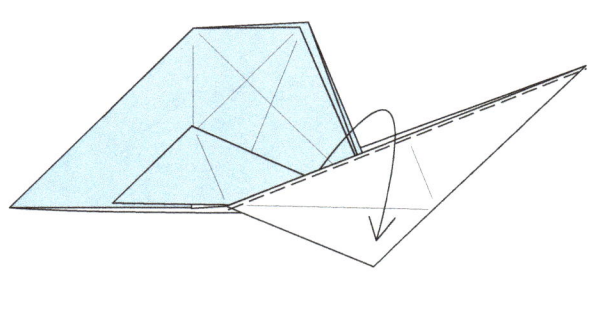

26. Pull out a single layer and wrap it around.

whale

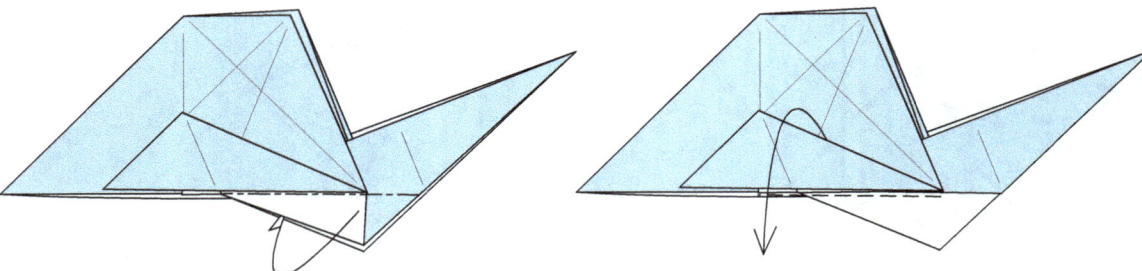

27. Mountain fold the corner inside.

28. Swing the top flap down.

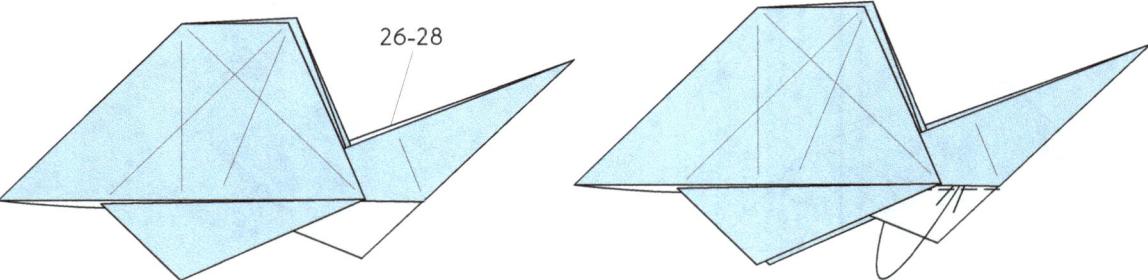

29. Repeat steps 26-28 behind.

30. Mountain fold the bottom flap inside to one side.

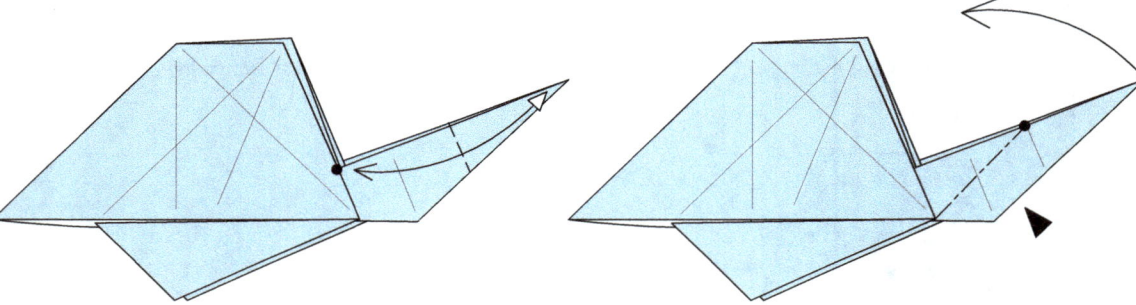

31. Precrease to the dotted corner.

32. Reverse fold the flap (closed reverse fold) using the dotted intersection.

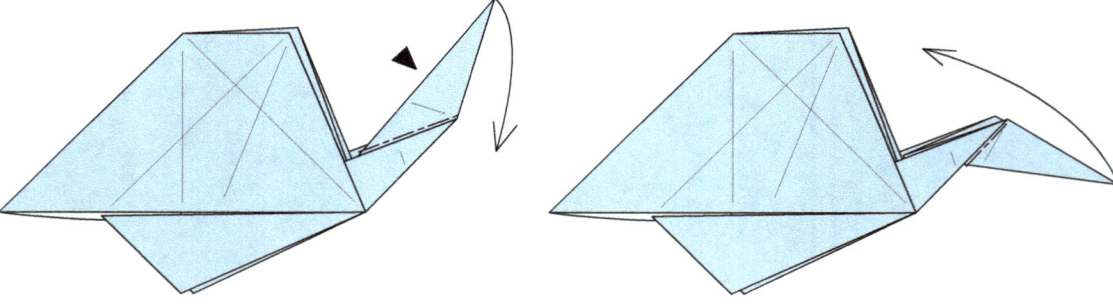

33. Reverse fold the flap down.

34. Reverse fold the flap up.

— whale —

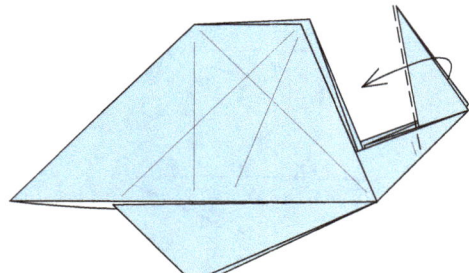

35. Lightly open out the flap.

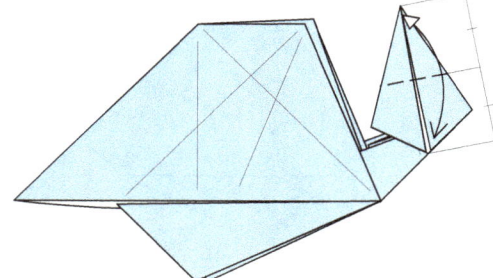

36. Precrease the flap in half.

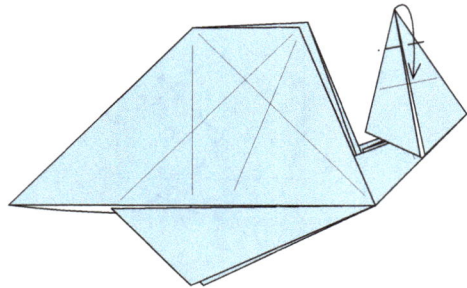

37. Valley fold to the last crease.

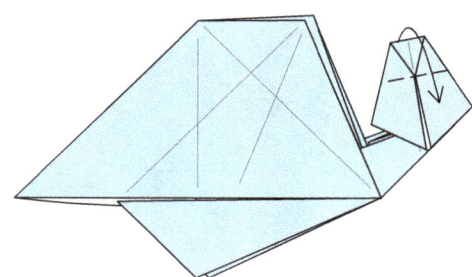

38. Valley fold along the existing crease.

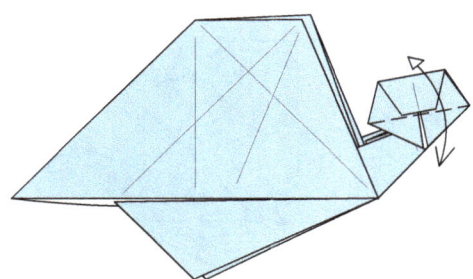

39. Precrease between the corners.

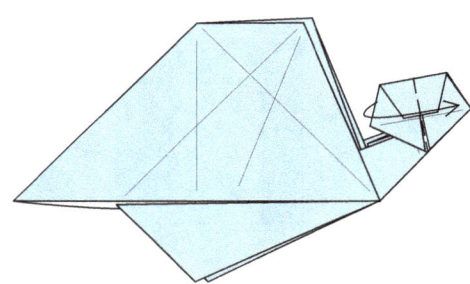

40. Close the flap back up.

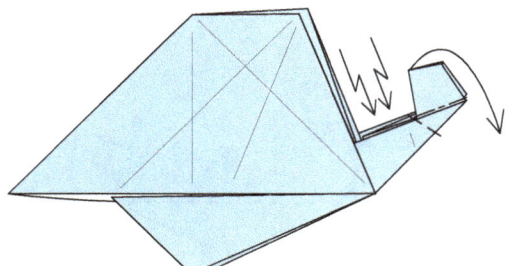

41. Crimp the flap down so its top edge lies straight.

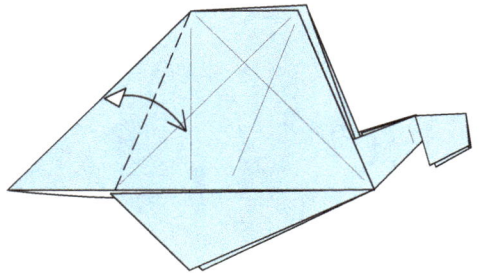

42. Precrease along the angle bisector.

whale

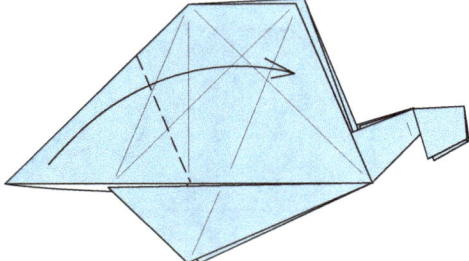

43. Valley fold over.

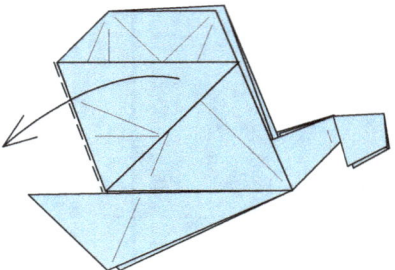

44. Unfold the flap.

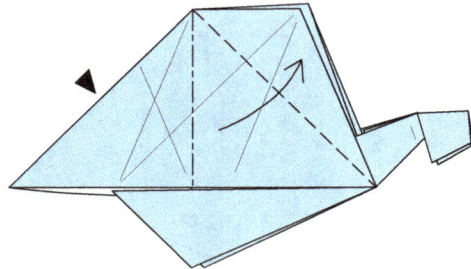

45. Lightly squash fold the flap.

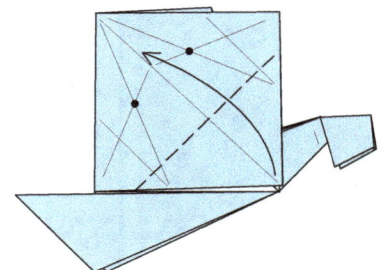

46. Valley fold so that the side edges hit the dotted intersections.

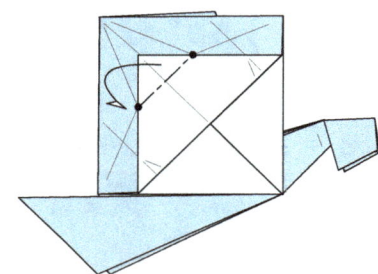

47. Mountain fold between the dotted intersections.

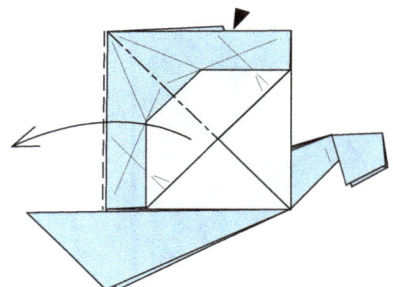

48. Squash fold the flap back over.

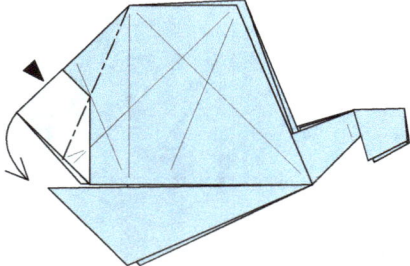

49. Reverse fold along the angle bisector.

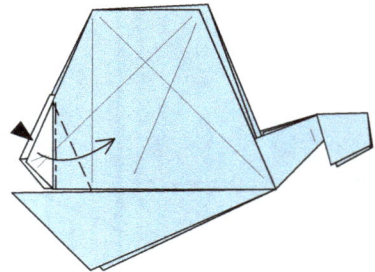

50. Squash fold the corner over.

whale

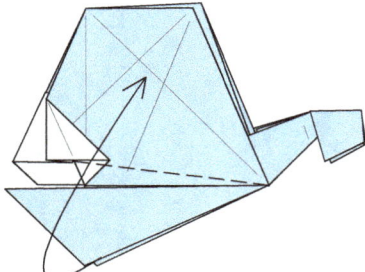

51. Valley fold the bottom section up.

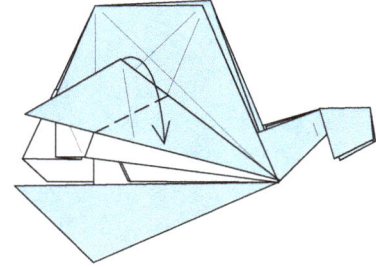

52. Valley fold the flap down.

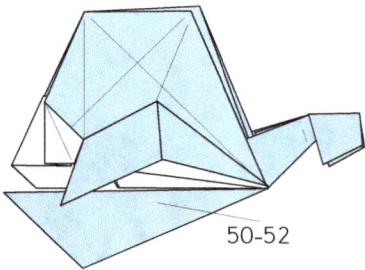

53. Repeat steps 50-52 behind.

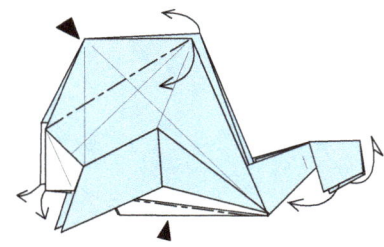

54. Open out the tail. Spread apart the top and bottom corners and softly squash fold the opposite sides into a 3-D shape.

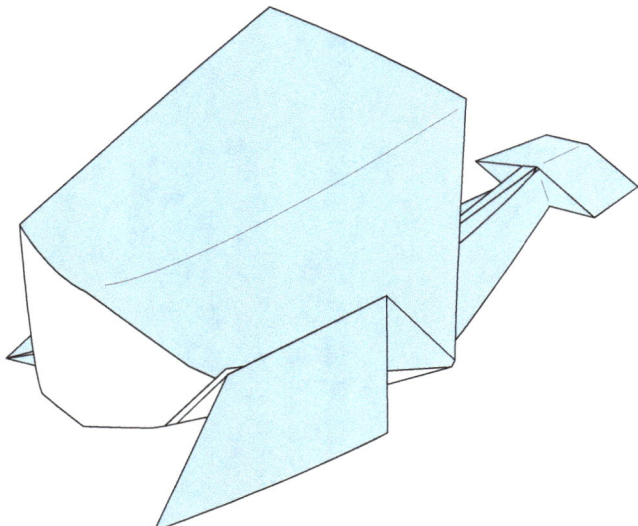

55. Completed *Whale*.

83

Lobster

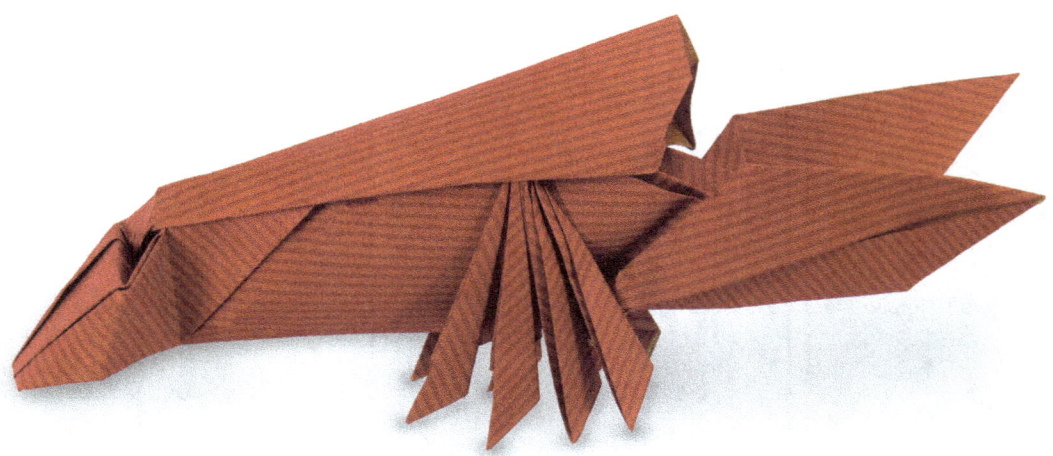

lobster

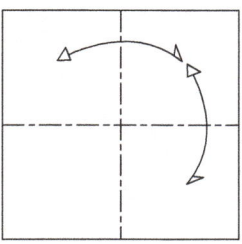

1. Precrease in half with mountain folds.

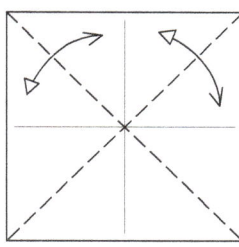

2. Precrease along the diagonals.

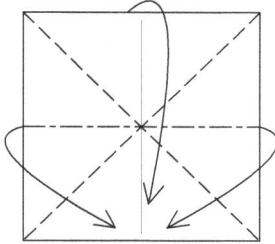

3. Fold in half while reverse folding the sides.

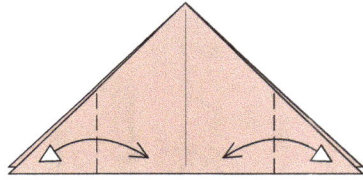

4. Precrease the sides in half.

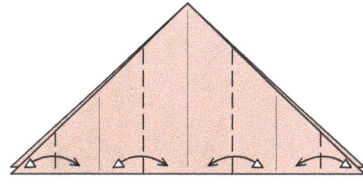

5. Precrease each section in half.

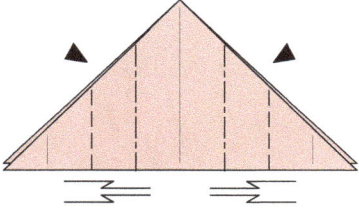

6. Reverse fold the flaps in and out.

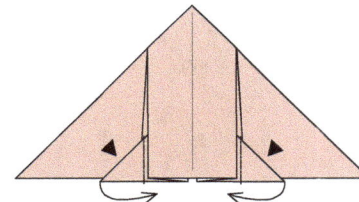

7. Reverse fold the tips inward.

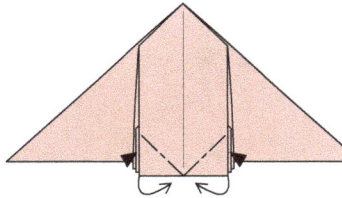

8. Reverse fold the top set of corners.

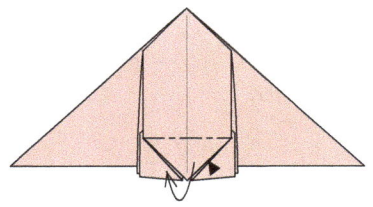

9. Reverse fold the resulting flap inside.

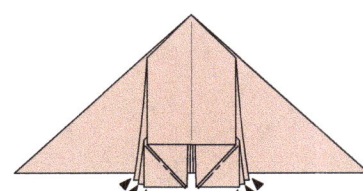

10. Reverse fold the three sets of corners.

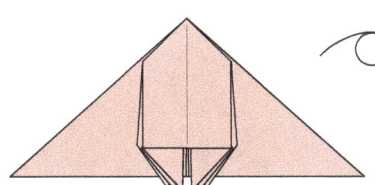

11. Turn over.

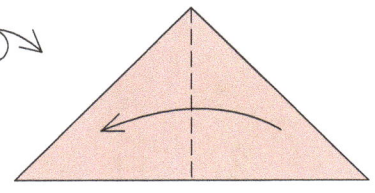

12. Swing over one flap.

lobster

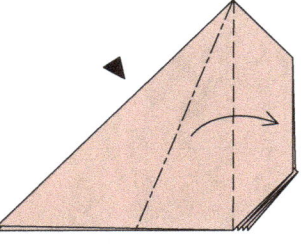

13. Squash fold the flap.

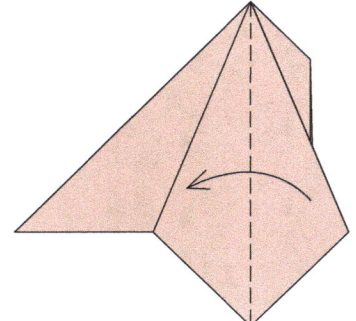

14. Swing over one flap.

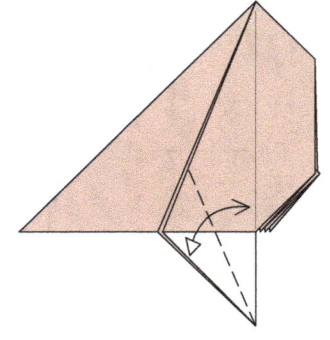

15. Precrease along the angle bisector.

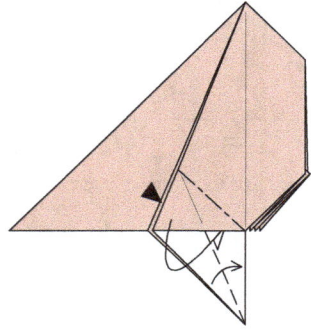

16. Reverse fold along the angle bisector.

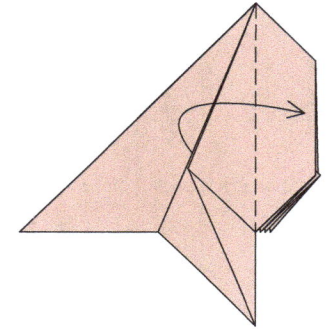

17. Swing over two flaps.

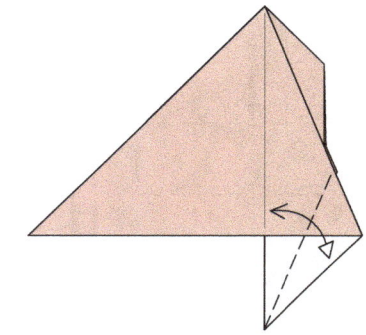

18. Precrease along the angle bisector.

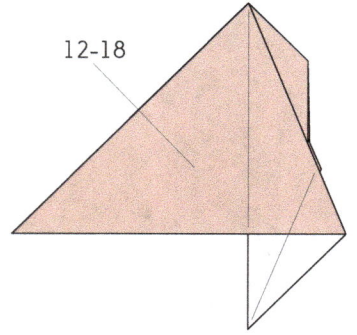

19. Repeat steps 12-18 in mirror image.

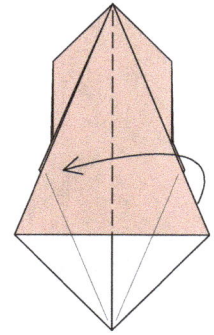

20. Swing over two flaps.

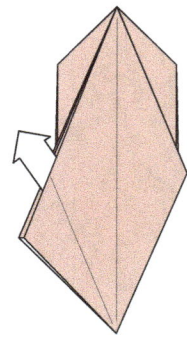

21. Pull out the middle layer.

lobster

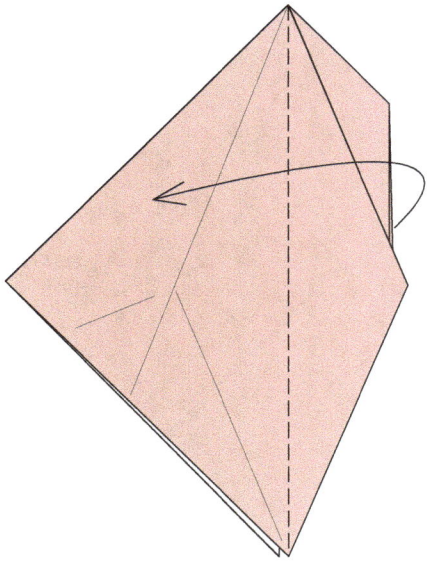

22. Valley fold the remaining layers over.

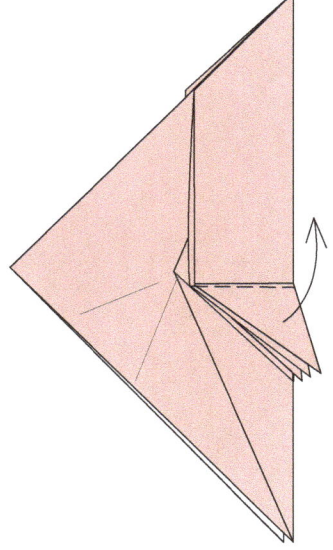

23. Swing one flap up.

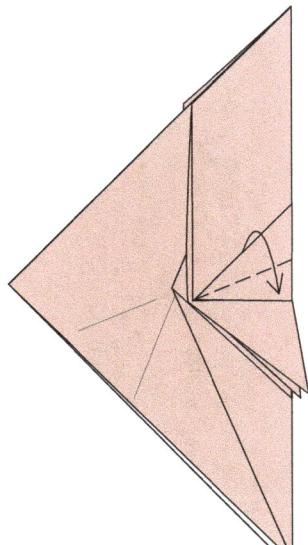

24. Valley fold along the angle bisector.

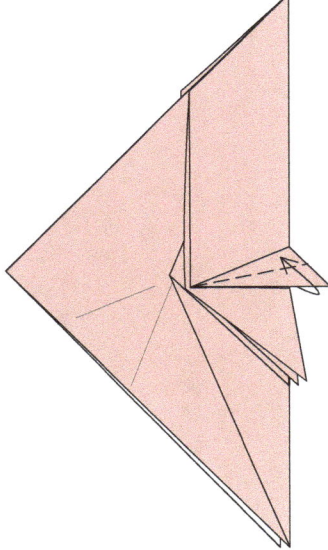

25. Valley fold up along the angle bisector.

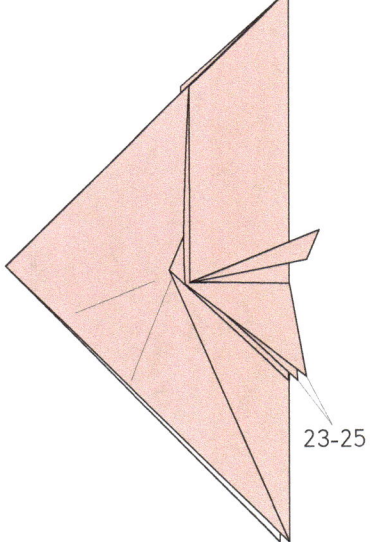

26. Repeat steps 23-25 on the next two sets of flaps.

lobster

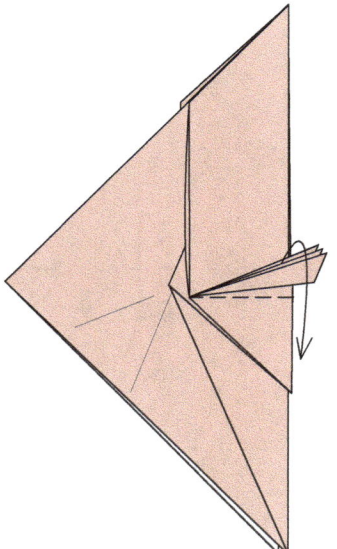

27. Swing two flaps down.

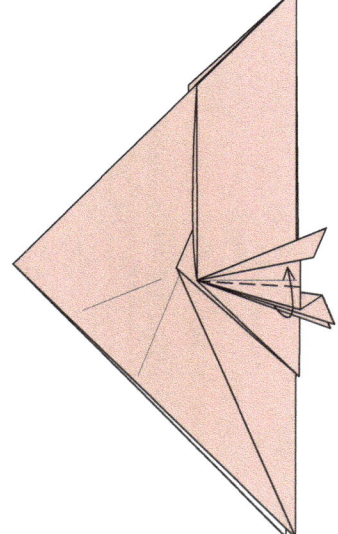

28. Valley fold the flap up, leaving a small gap between it and the flap above.

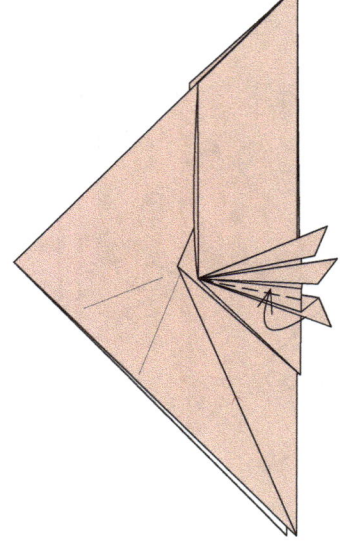

29. Valley fold the top layer, allowing the flap to flip around.

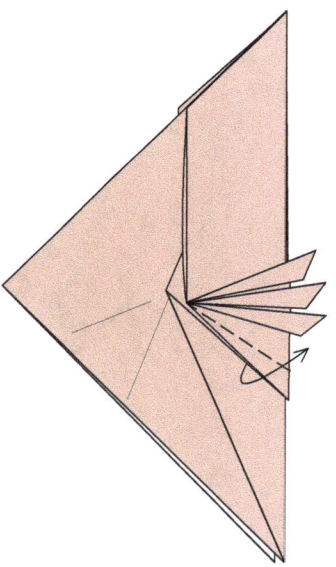

30. Valley fold the flap up, leaving a small gap.

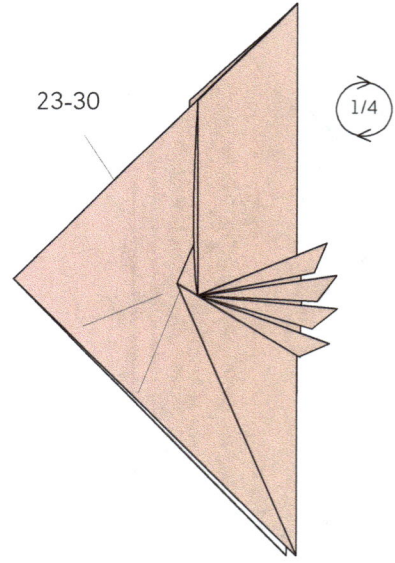

31. Repeat steps 23-30 behind. Rotate the model.

lobster

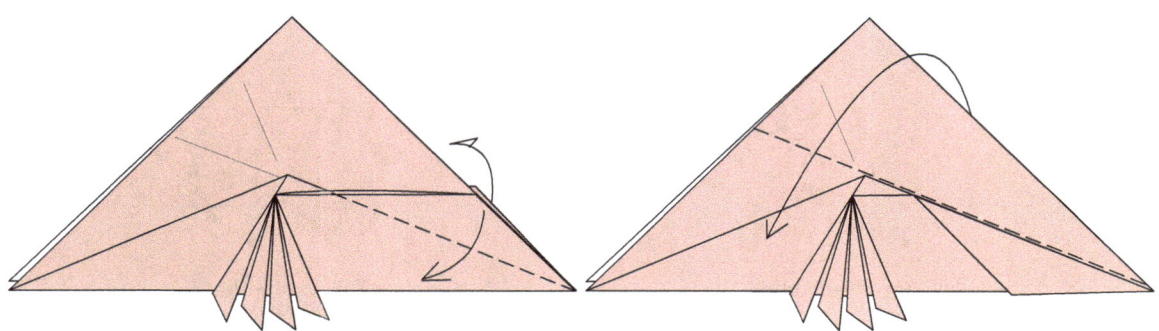

32. Valley fold the outer flaps along the angle bisectors.

33. Valley fold down.

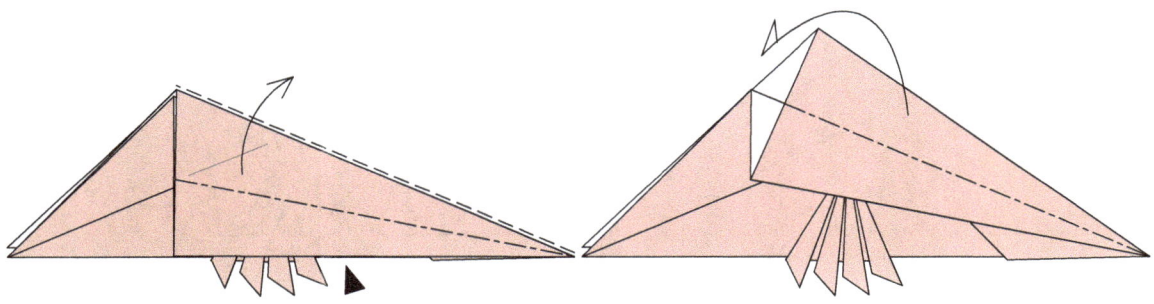

34. Squash fold along the angle bisector.

35. Mountain fold behind.

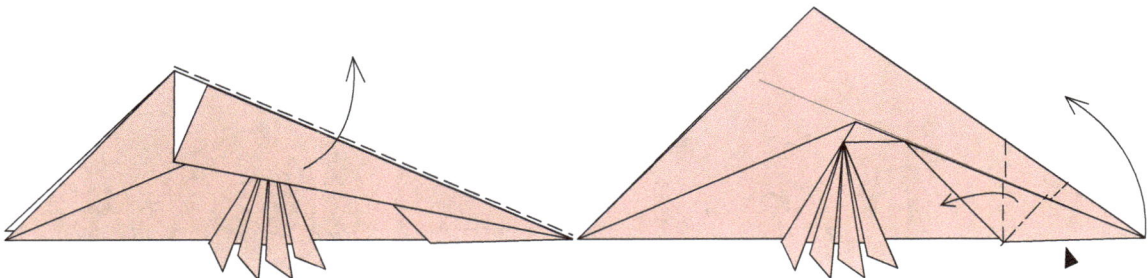

36. Swing the top flap up.

37. Squash fold the flap up.

lobster

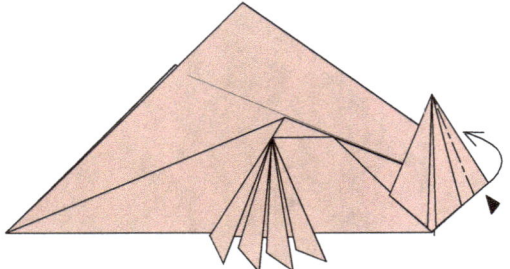

38. Reverse fold along the hidden thickness of the flap.

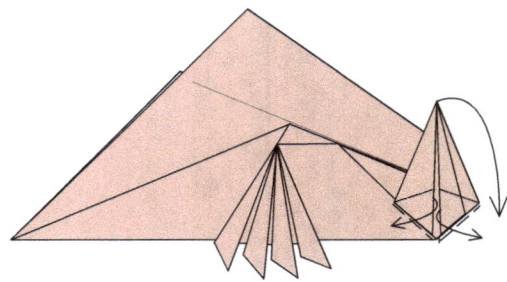

39. Swing the flap down while spreading apart the sides.

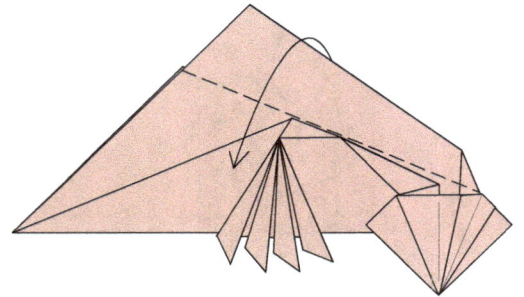

40. Valley fold the flap back down.

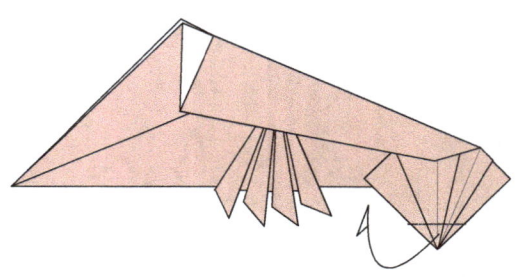

41. Mountain fold the tip inside.

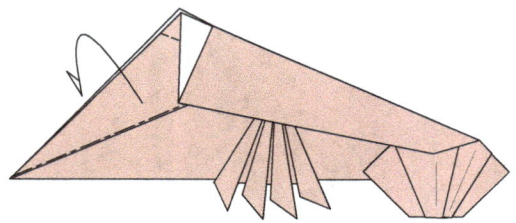

42. Mountain fold along the angle bisector, allowing a squash fold to form.

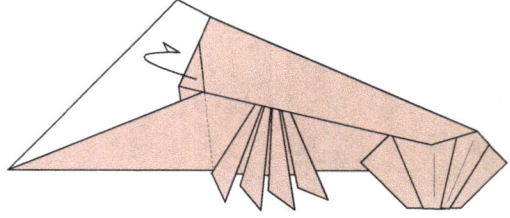

43. Mountain fold the edge inside.

lobster

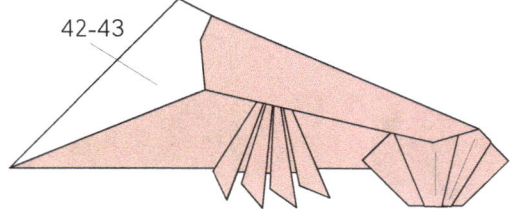

44. Repeat steps 42-43 behind.

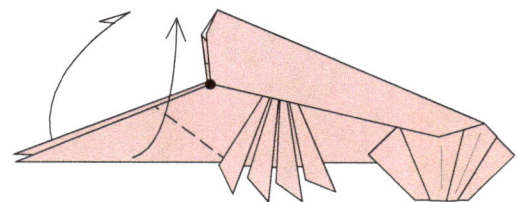

45. Valley fold the flaps up so the edges hit the dotted intersection.

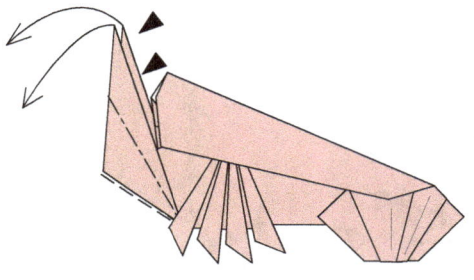

46. Squash fold the flaps down asymmetrically.

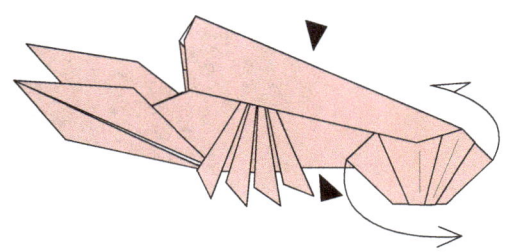

47. Round out the body and open out the tail section.

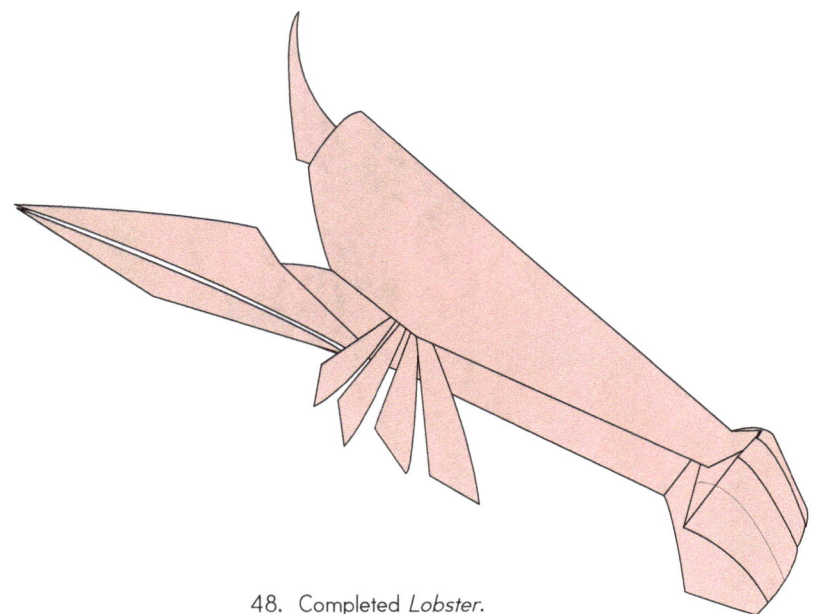

48. Completed *Lobster*.

Starfish

starfish

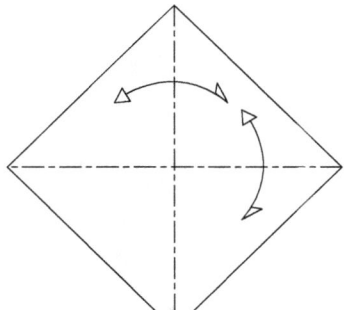

1. Precrease along the diagonals with mountain folds.

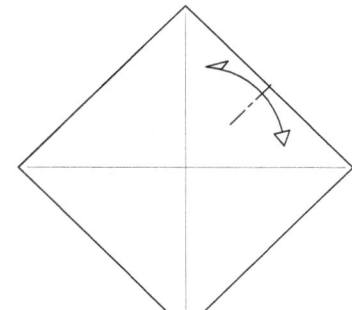

2. Pinch the edge in half with a mountain fold.

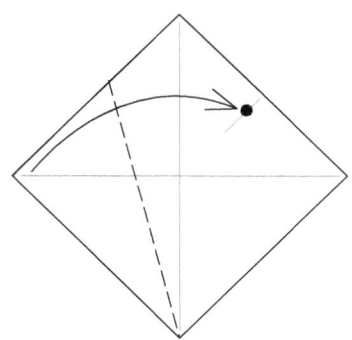

3. Valley fold the corner to the dotted crease.

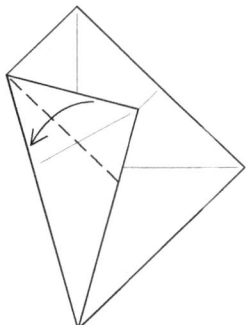

4. Valley fold along the angle bisector.

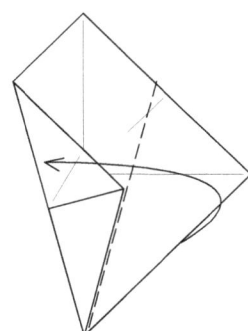

5. Valley fold towards the opposite edge.

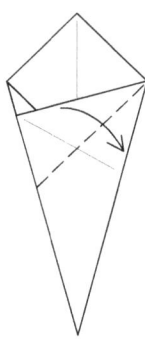

6. Valley fold along the angle bisector.

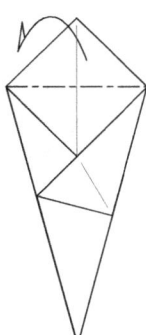

7. Mountain fold the corner behind.

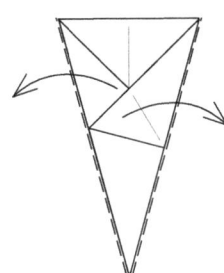

8. Open out the sides.

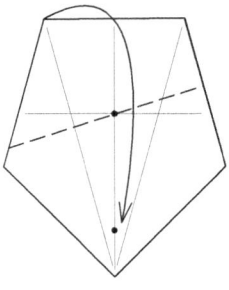

9. Valley fold the corner to the dotted crease, ensuring the fold passes through the dotted center.

starfish

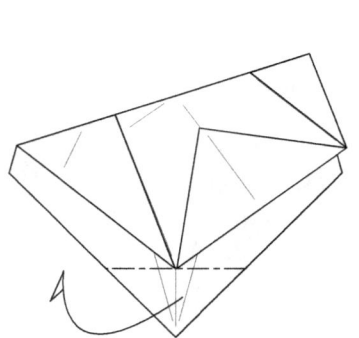

10. Mountain fold the corner behind.

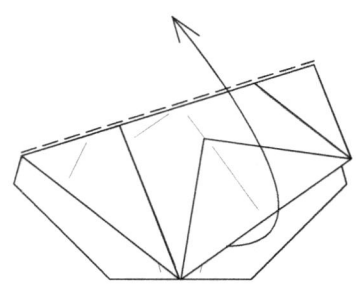

11. Open out the top flap.

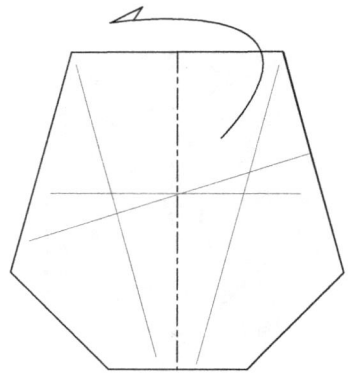

12. Mountain fold in half.

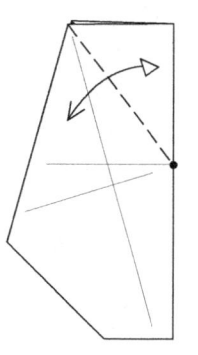

13. Precrease using the dotted intersection (this is *not* an angle bisector). Rotate the model.

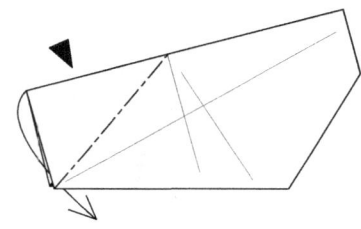

14. Reverse fold the corner.

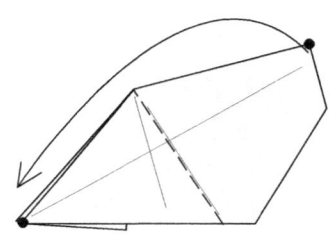

15. Valley fold the dotted corners to each other.

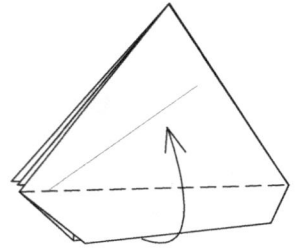

16. Valley fold the top layer up.

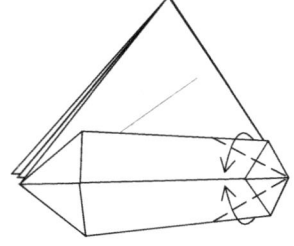

17. Valley fold along the angle bisectors.

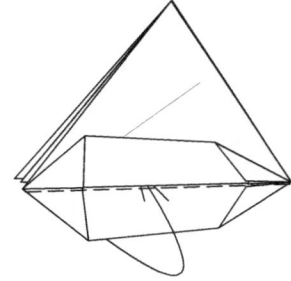

18. Tuck the bottom edge inside.

starfish

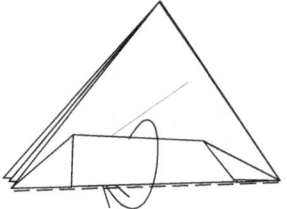

19. Tuck the top edge inside.

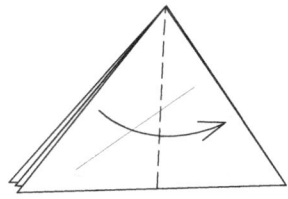

20. Valley fold the top layer.

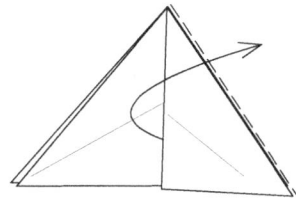

21. Raise the top layer.

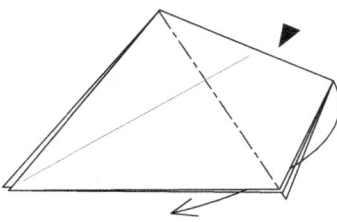

22. Reverse fold, allowing the flap from behind to fall in the center.

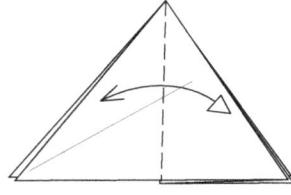

23. Swing the top flap over and then back.

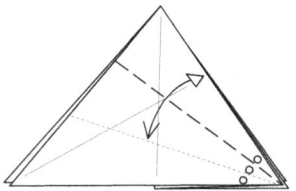

24. Precrease along the indicated angle trisector.

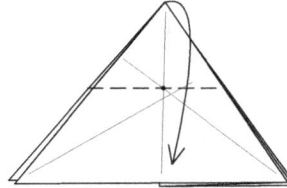

25. Valley fold through the dotted intersection of creases.

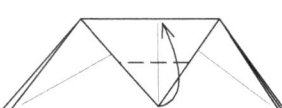

26. Valley fold the corner to the top.

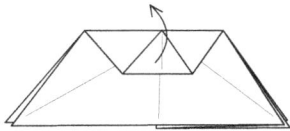

27. Unfold the pleat.

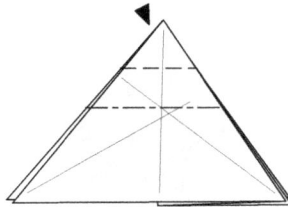

28. Sink the flap in and out along the existing creases.

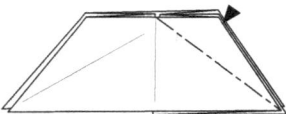

29. Closed sink the flap, leaving more layers distributed towards the back of the flap.

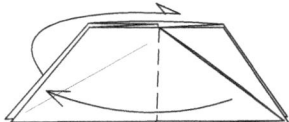

30. Swing over a flap at the front and at the rear.

starfish

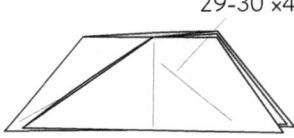

31. Repeat steps 29-30 four more times.

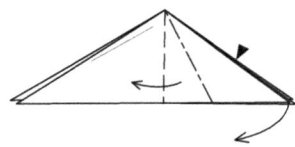

32. Squash fold the flap, leaving more layers distributed towards the left side of the flap.

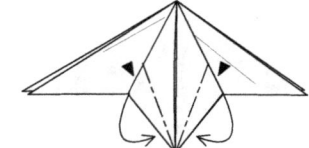

33. Reverse fold the sides.

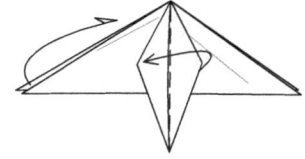

34. Swing over a flap at the front and at the rear.

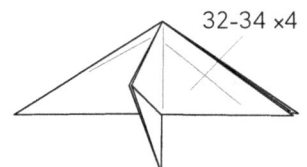

35. Repeat steps 32-34 four more times.

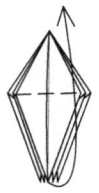

36. Swing up the top flap.

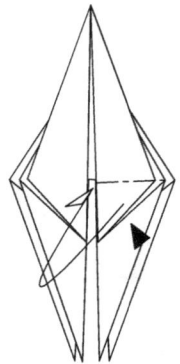

37. Reverse fold The corner inside.

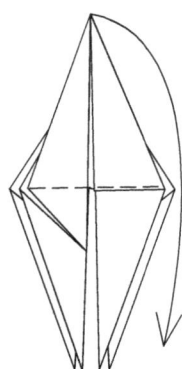

38. Swing the flap back down.

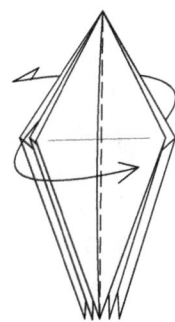

39. Swing over a flap at the front and at the rear.

starfish

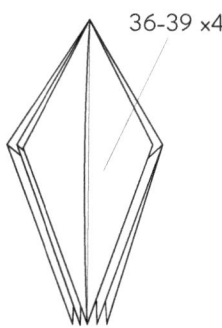

40. Repeat steps 36-39 four more times.

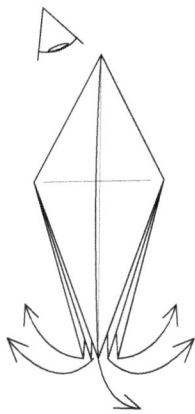

41. Spread apart the bottom flaps, leaving the top flap in a convex formation.

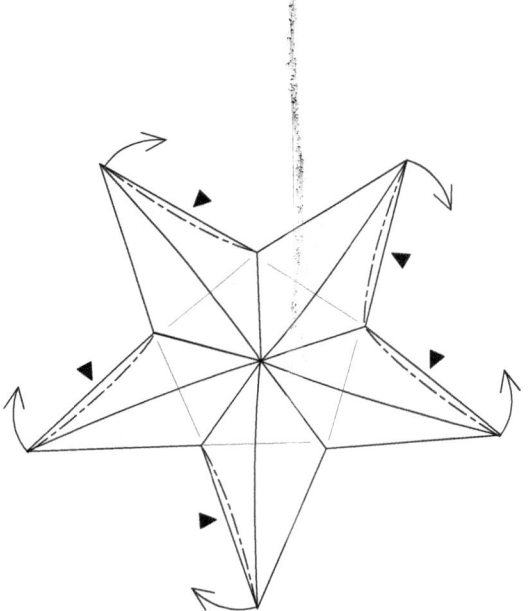

42. Curve one edge at each flap, allowing them to curl.

43. Completed *Starfish*.

Crab

crab

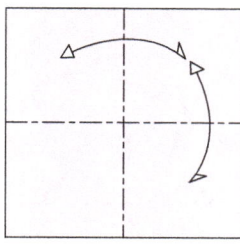

1. Precrease in half with mountain folds.

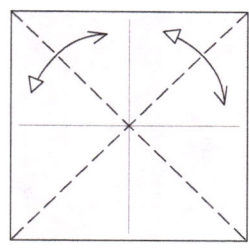

2. Precrease along the diagonals.

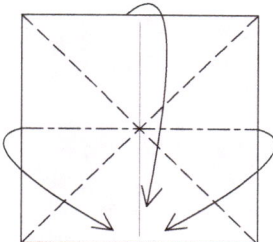

3. Fold in half while reverse folding the sides.

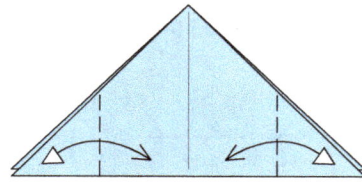

4. Precrease the sides in half.

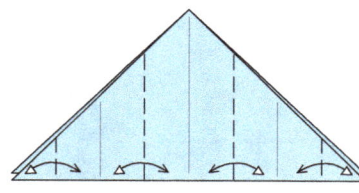

5. Precrease each section in half.

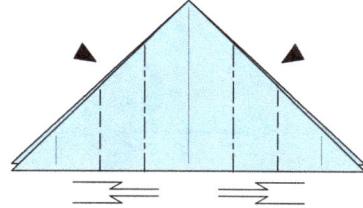

6. Reverse fold the flaps in and out.

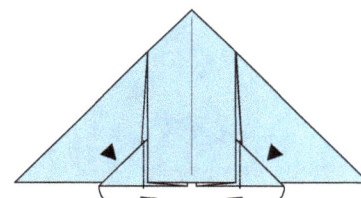

7. Reverse fold the tips inward.

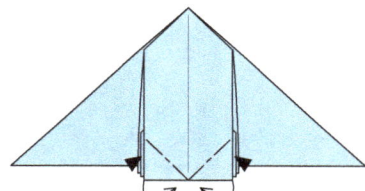

8. Reverse fold the top set of corners.

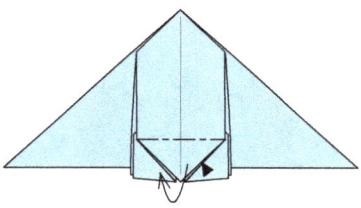

9. Reverse fold the resulting flap inside.

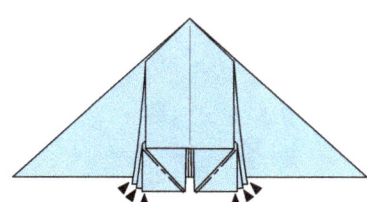

10. Reverse fold the three sets of corners.

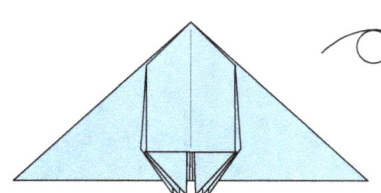

11. Turn over.

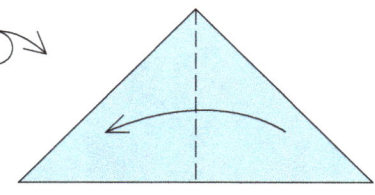

12. Swing over one flap.

— crab —

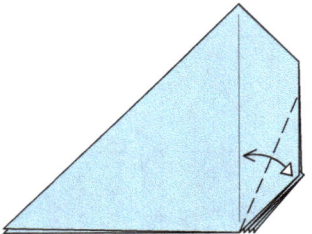

13. Precrease along the angle bisector.

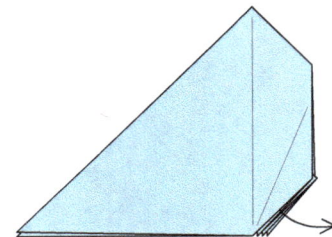

14. Undo the top reverse fold.

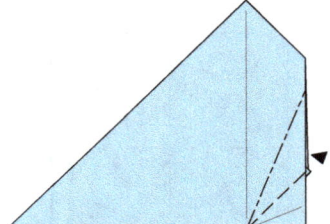

15. Reverse fold in and out along the existing creases.

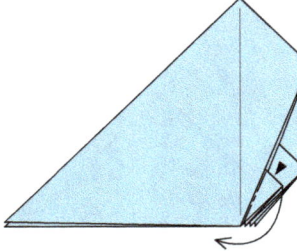

16. Reverse fold the small flap.

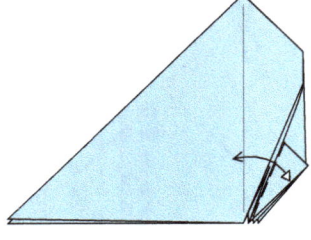

17. Precrease along the angle bisector.

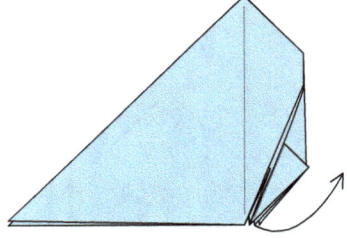

18. Pull out the corner.

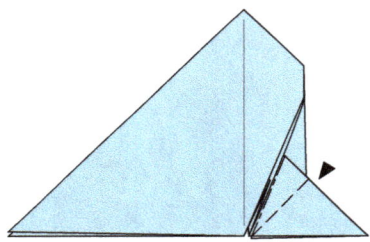

19. Reverse fold in and out along the existing creases.

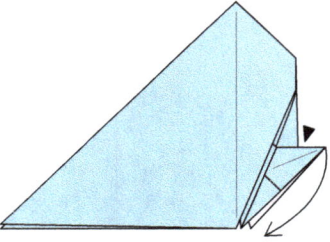

20. Reverse fold down.

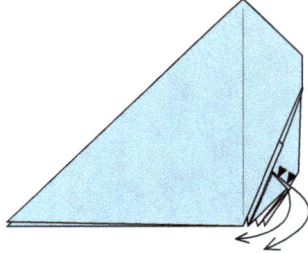

21. Reverse fold the two flaps.

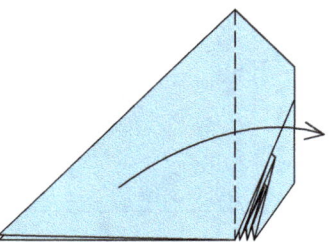

22. Swing the flap back over.

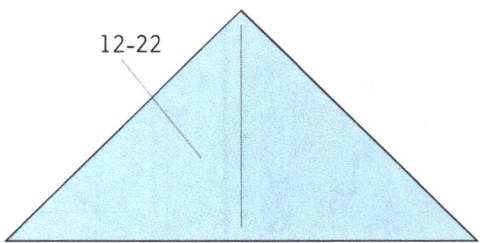

23. Repeat steps 12–22 in mirror image.

crab

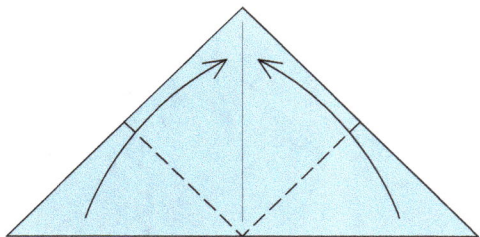

24. Valley fold the flaps up.

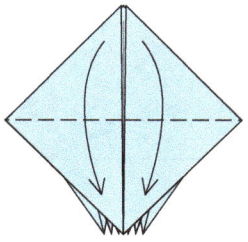

25. Valley fold the flaps down.

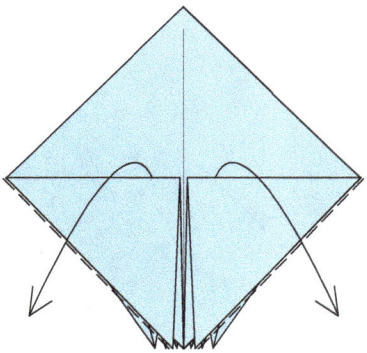

26. Swing the top layers outwards.

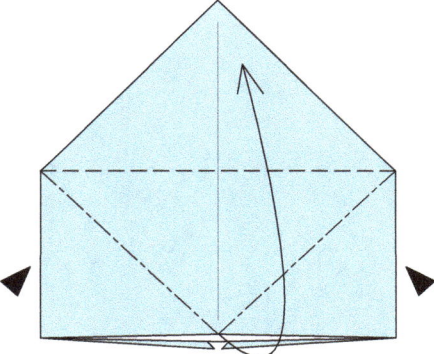

27. Bring the top layer up while squash folding the sides flat.

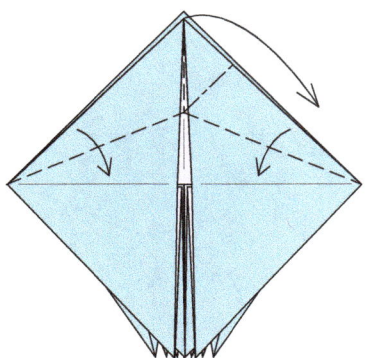

28. Rabbit ear the top flap.

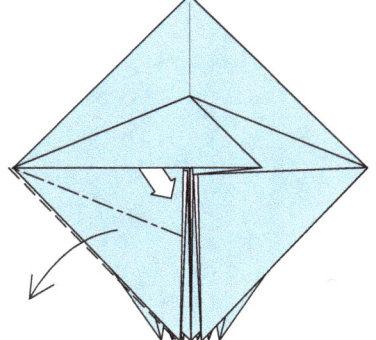

29. Pull out a single layer, squash folding the paper at the bottom.

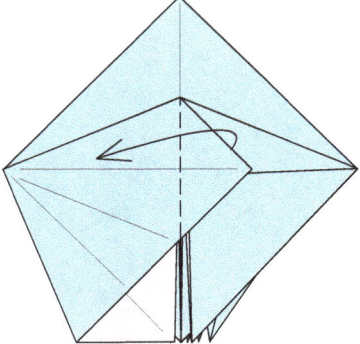

30. Swing over the center flap.

crab

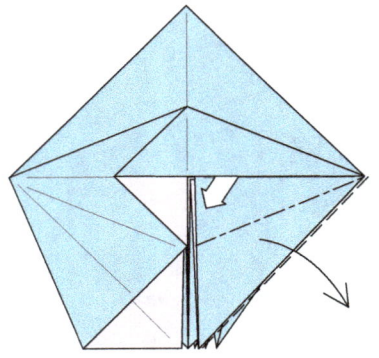

31. Pull out a single layer, squash folding the paper at the bottom.

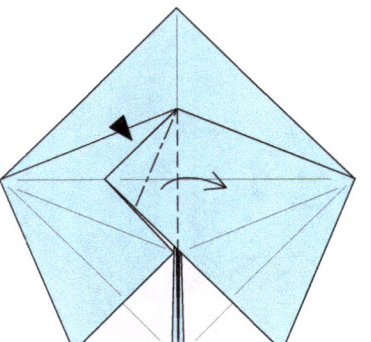

32. Squash fold the center flap.

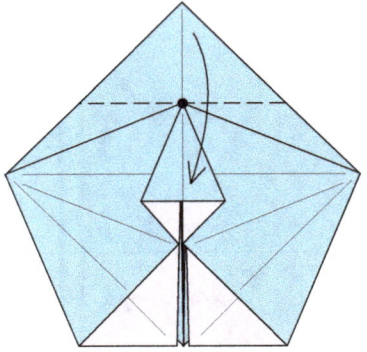

33. Valley fold down, noting the dotted intersection.

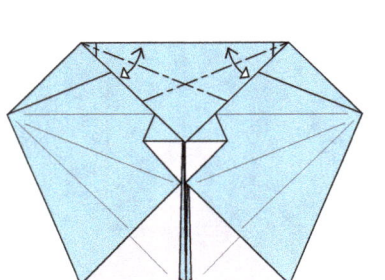

34. Precrease along the angle bisectors.

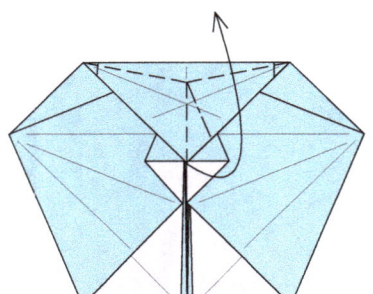

35. Rabbit ear along angle bisectors.

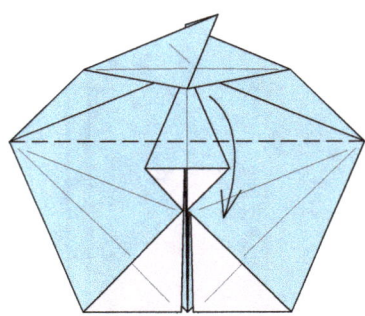

36. Swing the flap down.

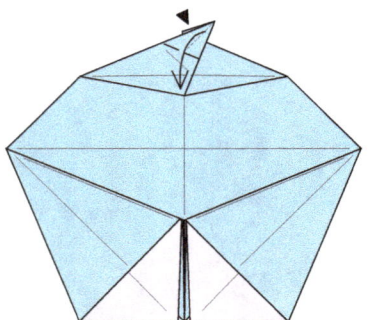

37. Fold the corner to the center, allowing a squash fold to form.

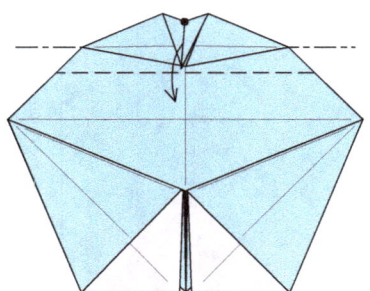

38. Pleat the top section downwards, such that the valley fold hits the dotted intersection.

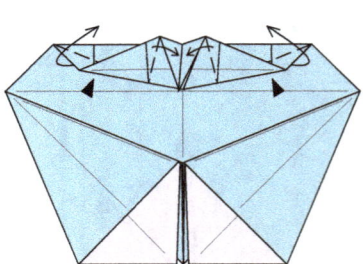

39. Valley fold to the top while swivel folding inwards.

crab

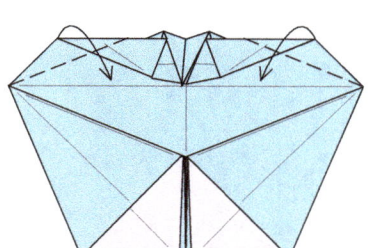

40. Valley fold along the angle bisectors.

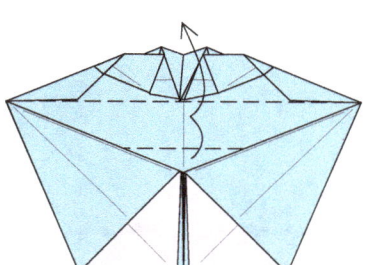

41. Valley fold over and over, allowing the two small points at the top to peek through.

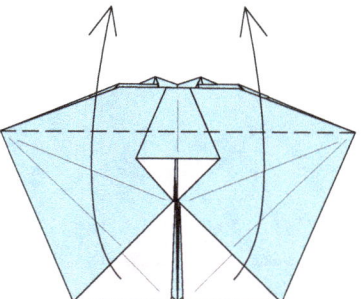

42. Swing the bottom flaps up.

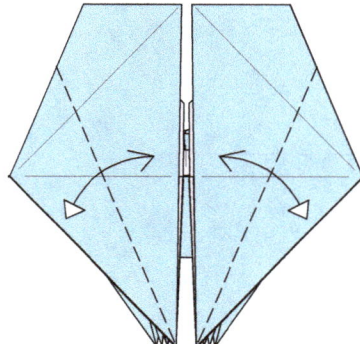

43. Precrease along the angle bisectors.

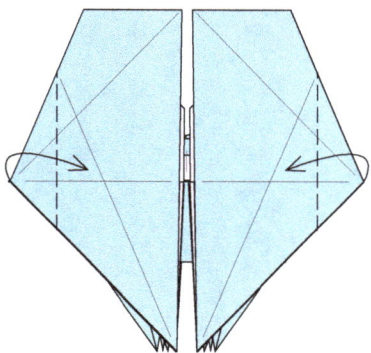

44. Valley fold to the last creases.

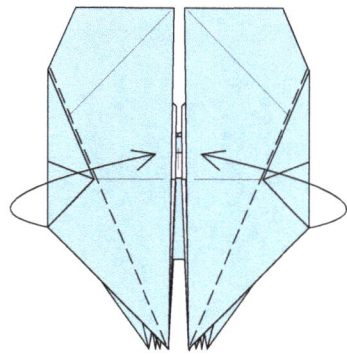

45. Valley fold along the existing creases.

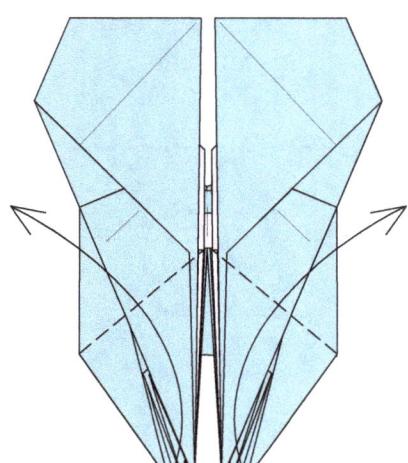

46. Valley fold the clusters of flaps outwards.

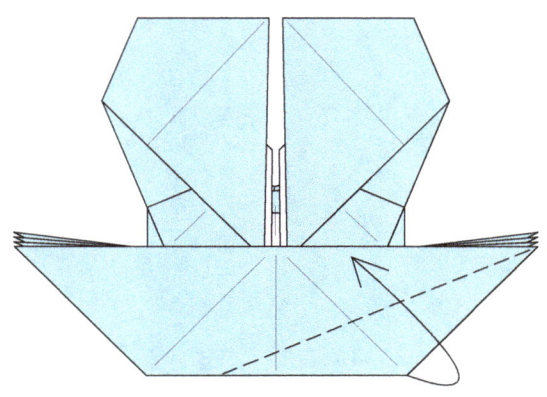

47. Valley fold along the angle bisector.

crab

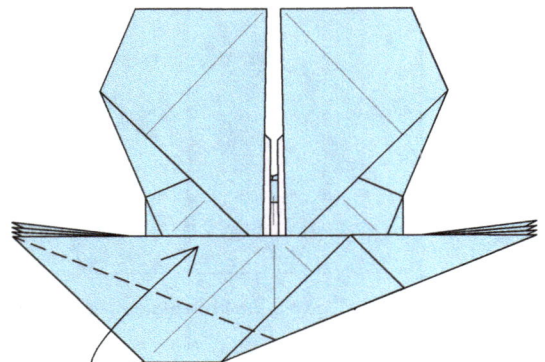

48. Valley fold the other side along the angle bisector.

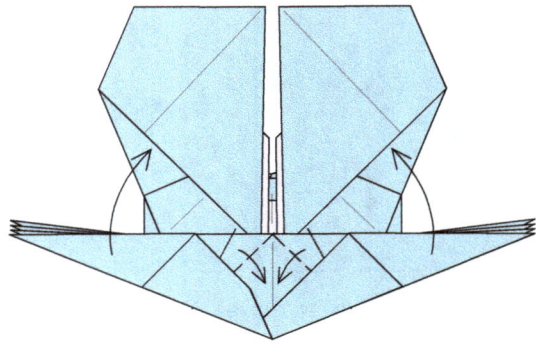

49. Slide the clusters of flaps up, allowing small pleats to form at the center.

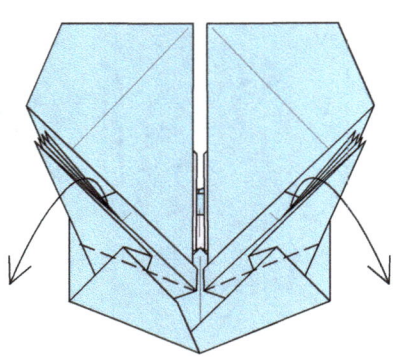

50. Valley fold the clusters of flaps outwards.

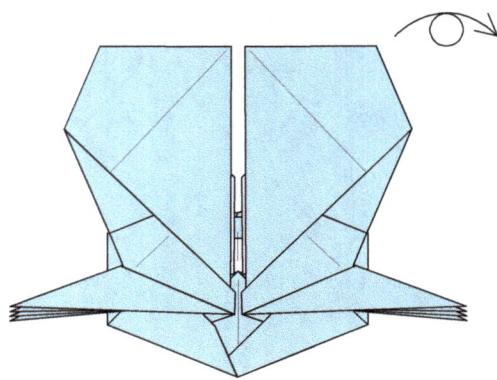

51. Turn over.

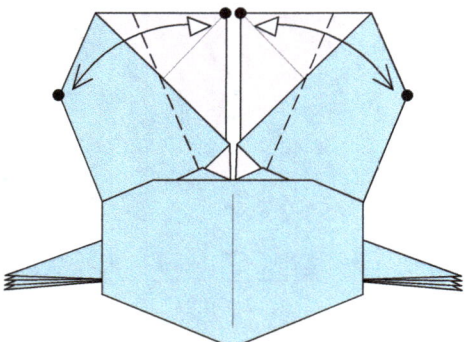

52. Precrease the top flaps.

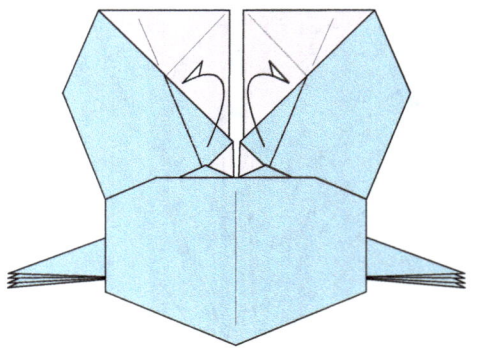

53. Mountain fold along the existing creases.

crab

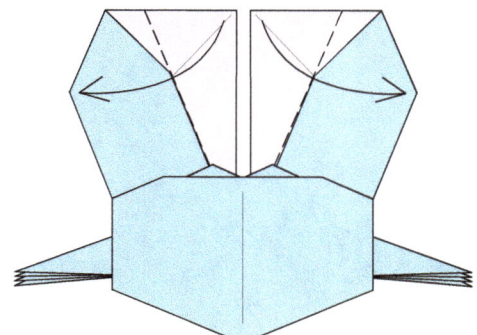

54. Valley fold along the existing creases.

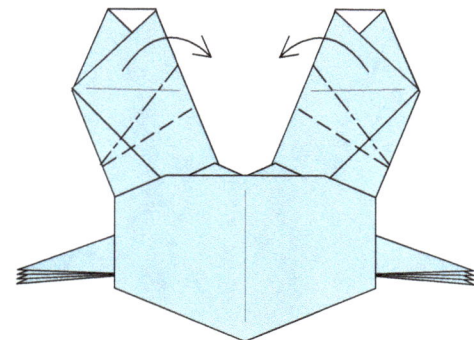

55. Pleat the flaps inwards.

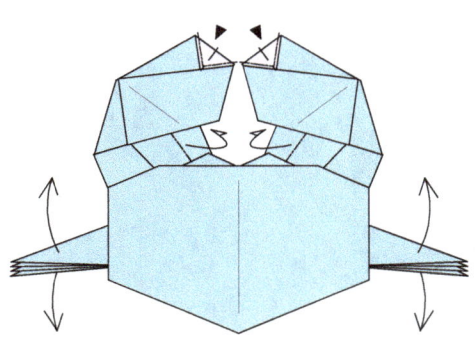

56. Shape the claws and spread apart the legs.

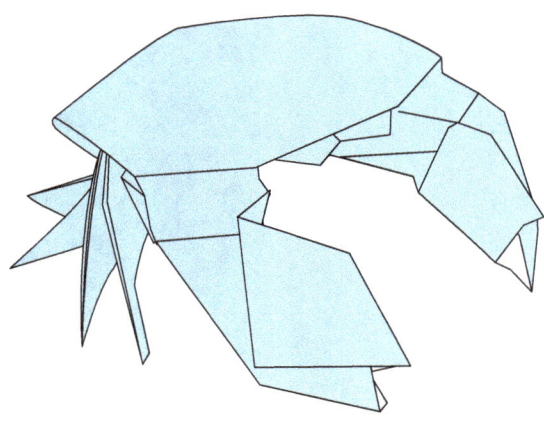

57. Completed *Crab*.

Seahorse

seahorse

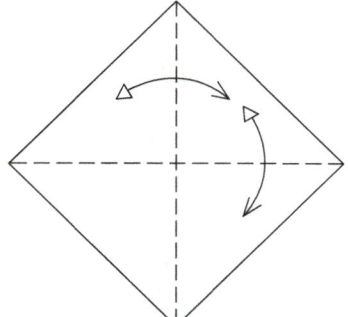

1. Precrease along the diagonals.

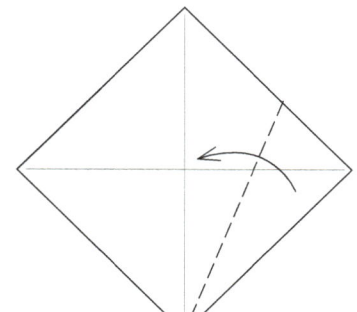

2. Valley fold to the center.

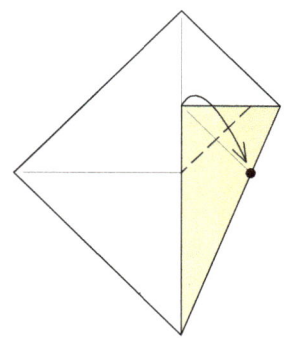

3. Valley fold to the dotted intersection.

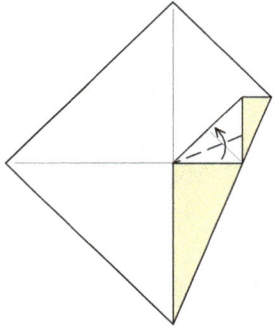

4. Valley fold along the angle bisector.

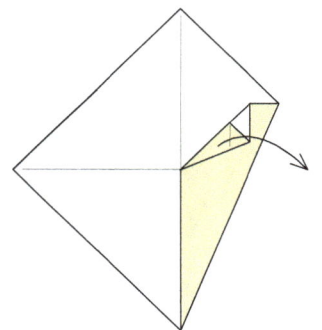

5. Unfold the pleat.

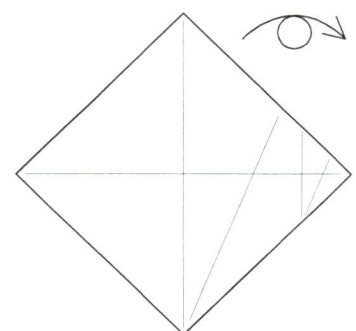

6. Turn over.

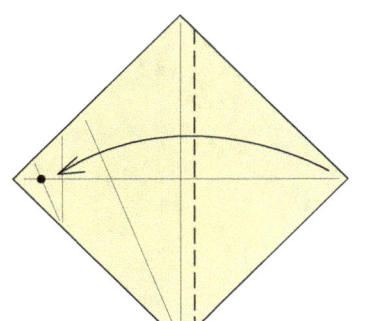

7. Valley fold to the dotted intersection of creases.

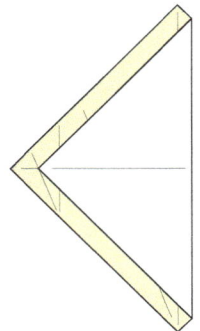

8. Turn over.

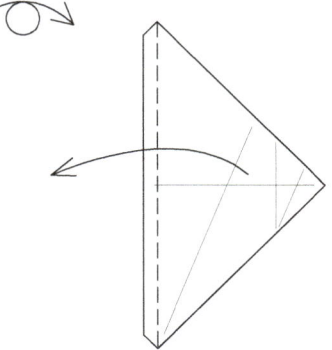

9. Valley fold along the existing crease.

seahorse

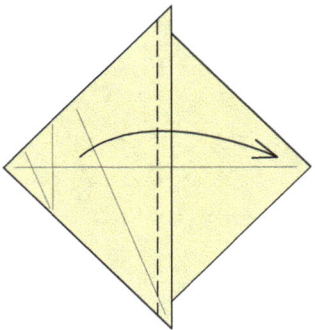

10. Valley fold over so the corners meet.

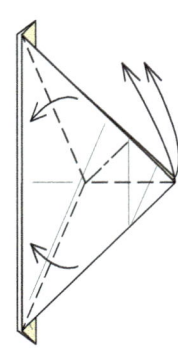

11. Rabbit ear both sides up.

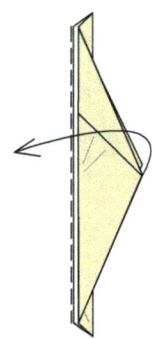

12. Swing over one flap.

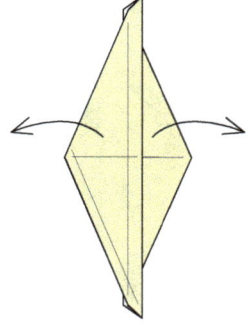

13. Pull apart the center pleat.

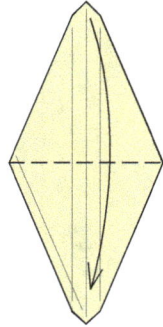

14. Valley fold down.

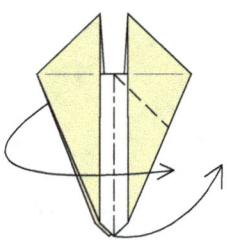

15. Fold in half while incorporating a reverse fold.

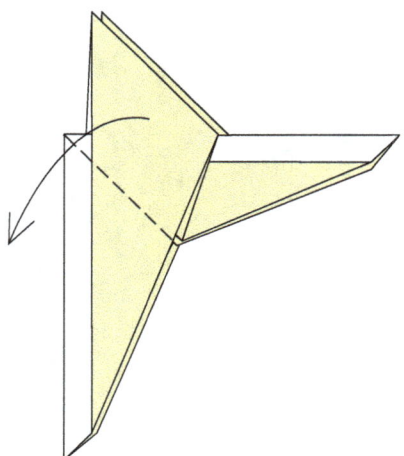

16. Valley fold the top flap over.

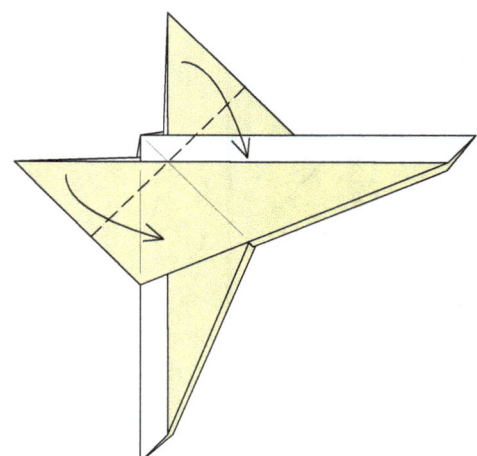

17. Valley fold the flaps down so they meet the edges.

seahorse

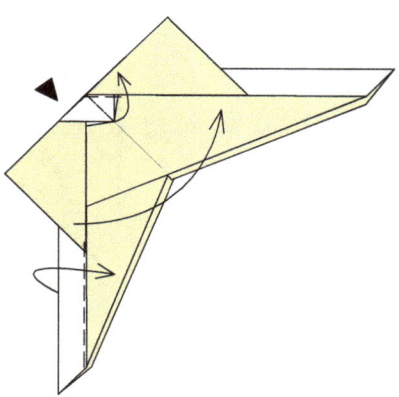

18. Valley fold the side edge over, pulling the top flap up.

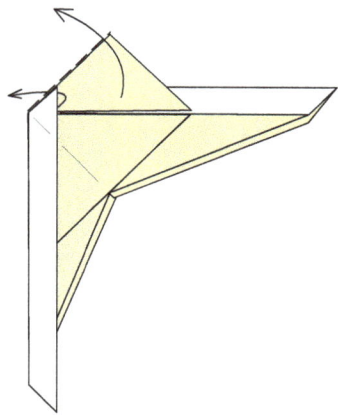

19. Swing the flap up, allowing a layer to be pulled out.

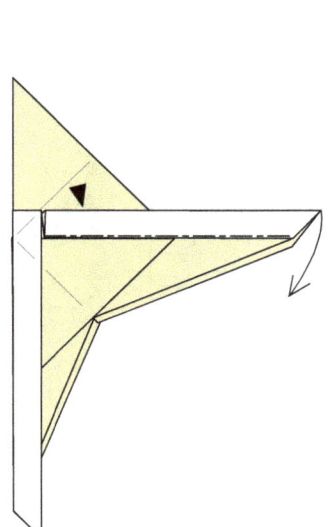

20. Reverse fold (like a closed sink) the top edge down.

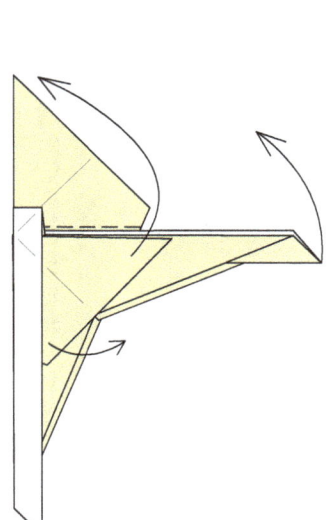

21. Rotate the cluster of flaps up.

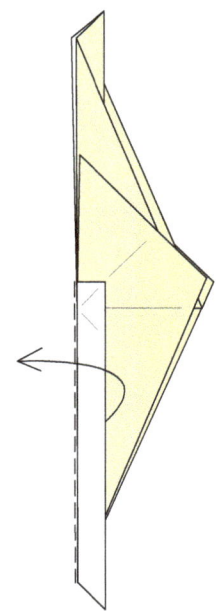

22. Swing the flap over.

seahorse

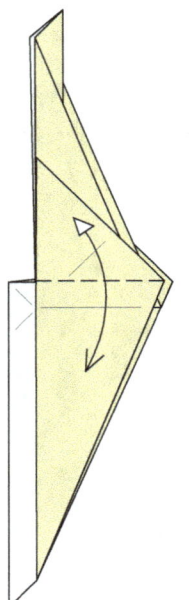 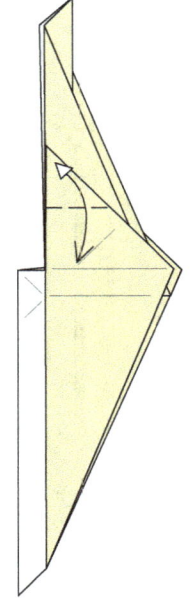 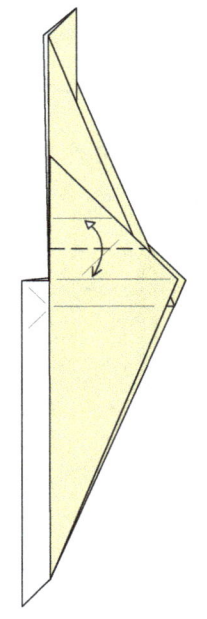 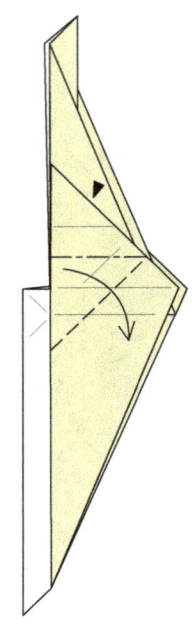

23. Precrease the top flap.

24. Precrease towards the last crease.

25. Precrease the middle area in half.

26. Squash fold along the existing creases. The corner should *not* meet the outer edge.

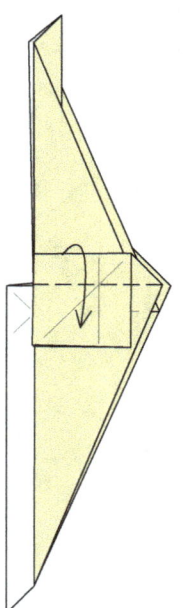 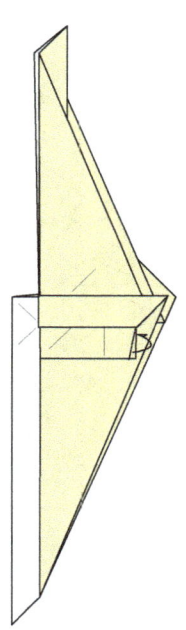 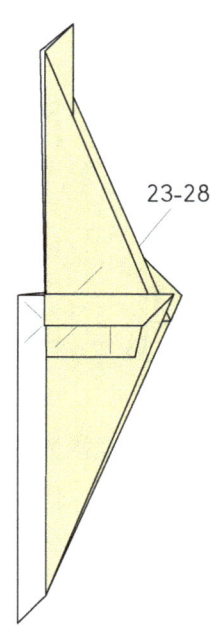 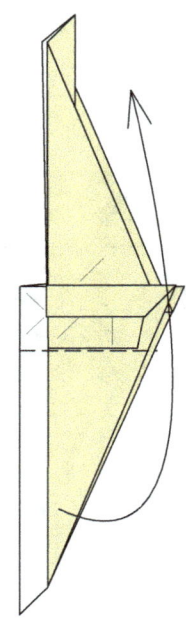

27. Valley fold the top edge down.

28. Mountain fold a small portion of the edge inside.

29. Repeat steps 23-28 behind.

30. Valley fold the flap up, aligning with the bottom edge of the middle flap.

110

seahorse

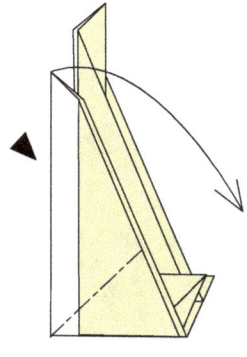

31. Squash fold the flap over.

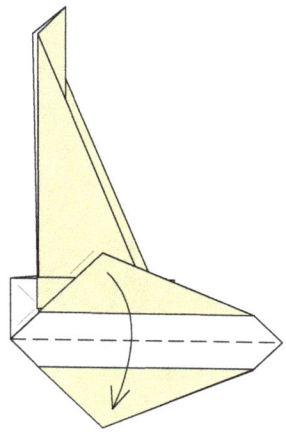

32. Valley fold the flap in half.

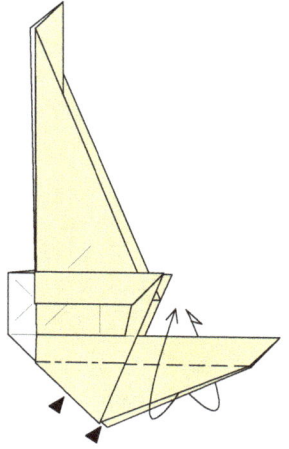

33. Reverse fold the sides up.

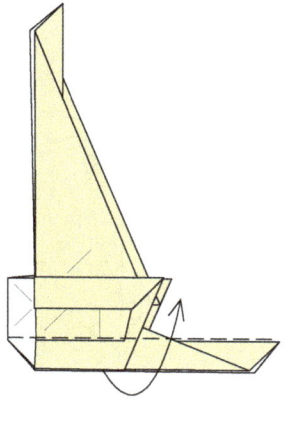

34. Spread open the bottom flap.

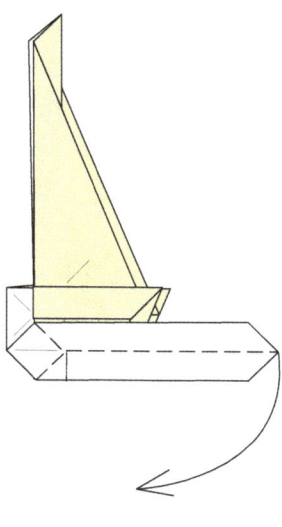

35. Rabbit ear down, allowing the trapped layer to get pulled down.

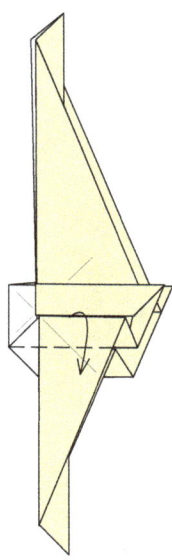

36. Swing the edge down.

111

seahorse

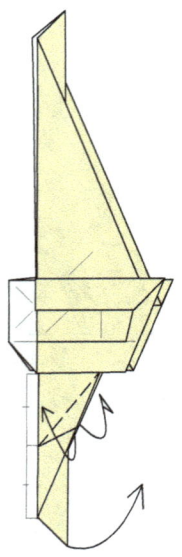

37. Crimp the flap up so the bottom corner sticks out straight.

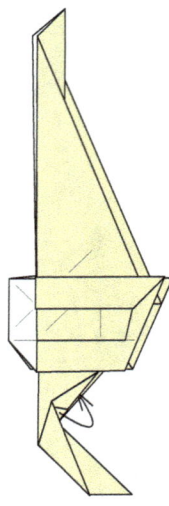

38. Tuck the layer inside.

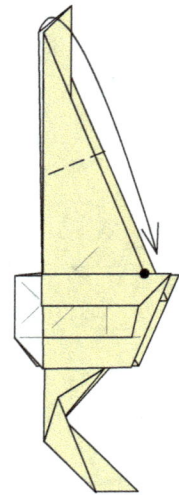

39. Valley fold towards the dotted intersection.

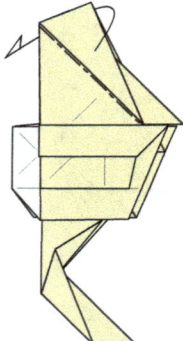

40. Mountain fold behind.

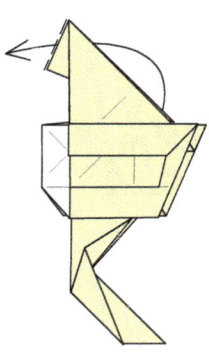

41. Swing the rear flap out.

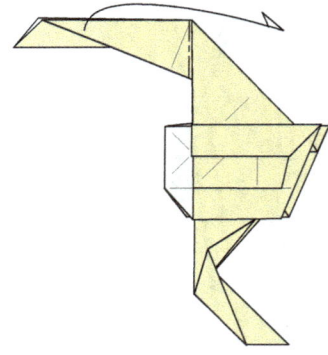

42. Mountain fold the flap over.

seahorse

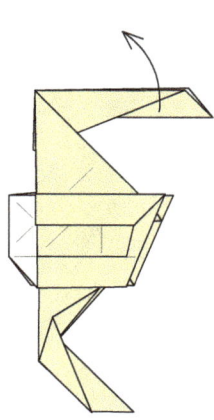
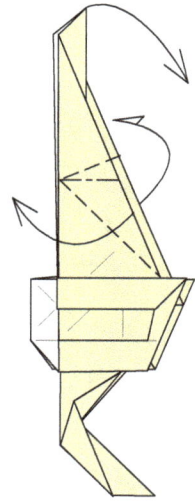
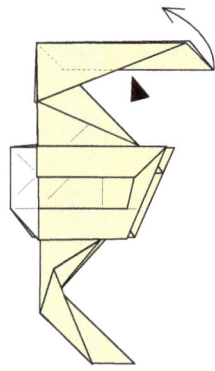

43. Unfold the pleat.

44. Crimp along the existing creases.

45. Sink the middle edge up.

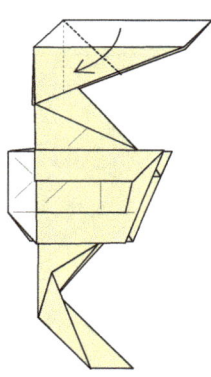
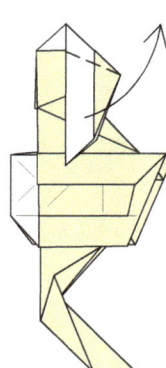
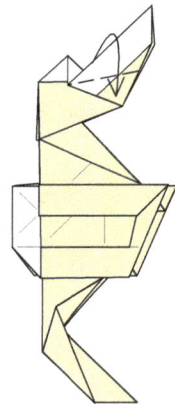

46. Valley fold towards the imaginary vertical line.

47. Valley fold so the top edge lies at a 45 degree angle.

48. Valley fold along the angle bisector.

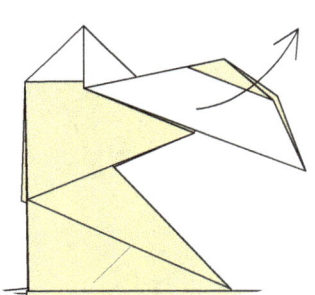
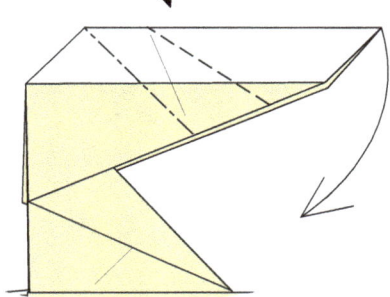
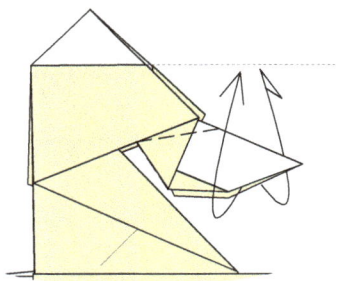

49. Unfold the pleat.

50. Reverse fold in and out along the existing creases.

51. Outside reverse fold towards the imaginary line.

seahorse

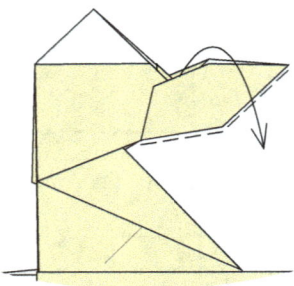

52. Open out the top. It will not lie flat.

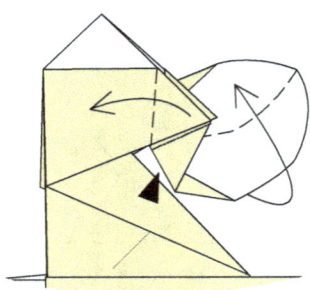

53. Close the flap back up while squash folding.

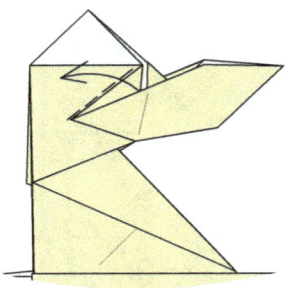

54. Pull out the trapped single layer and flatten.

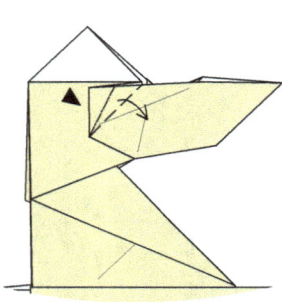

55. Squash fold the corner.

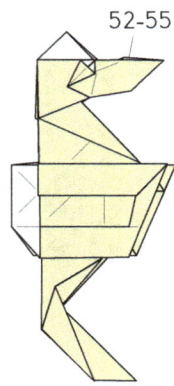

56. Repeat steps 52-55 behind.

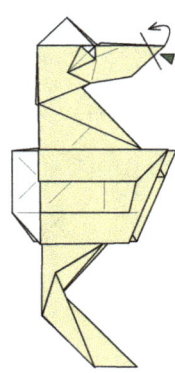

57. Reverse fold the corner.

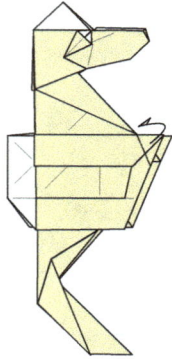

58. Mountain fold the corner inside.

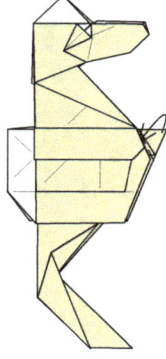

59. Tuck the corner into the pocket.

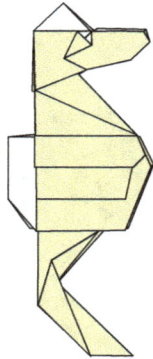

60. Completed *Seahorse*.

Octopus

octopus

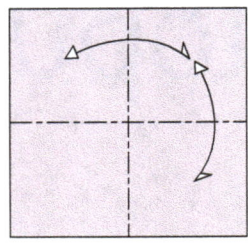 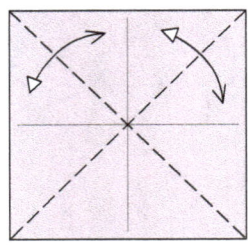 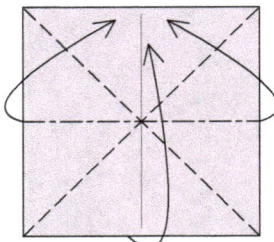

1. Precrease in half with mountain folds.
2. Precrease along the diagonals.
3. Fold in half while reverse folding the sides.

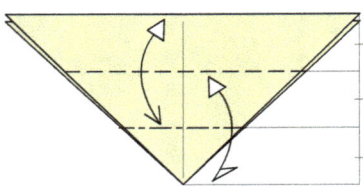 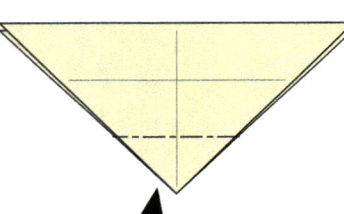 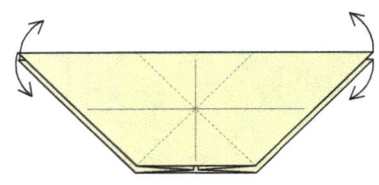

4. Pleat into thirds and unfold.
5. Sink the corner.
6. Rotate the flaps in opposite directions, causing the center sink to spread apart.

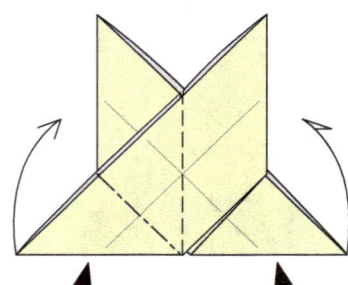 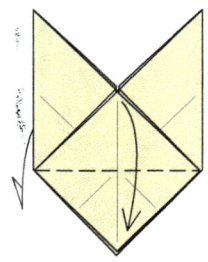 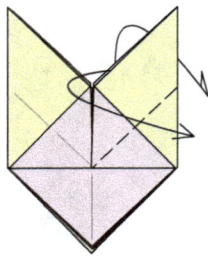

7. Squash fold the side flaps up.
8. Valley fold the top layers down at each side.
9. Outside reverse fold the flap.

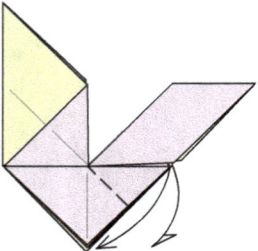 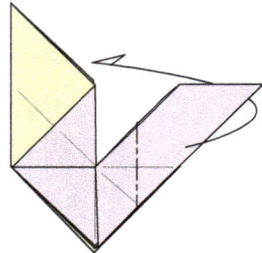 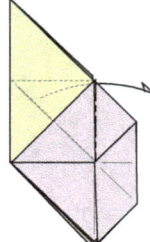

10. Pull out a trapped corner from each side and flatten.
11. Mountain fold the flap.
12. Mountain fold the flap from behind.

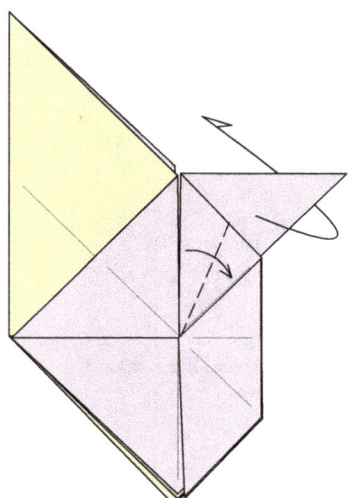

13. Valley fold along the angle bisector, allowing the flap from behind to flip forward.

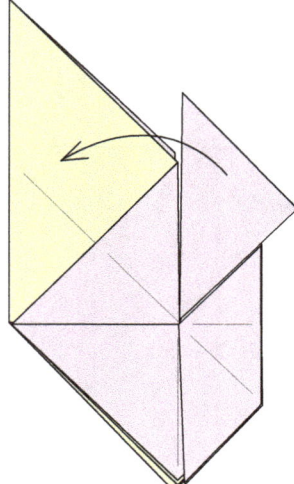

14. Unfold the pleat.

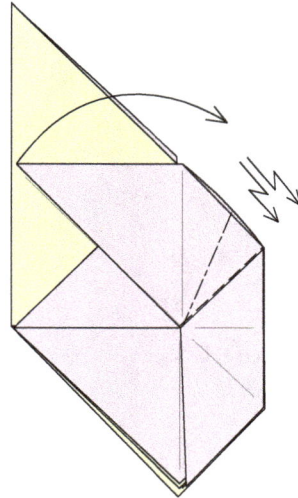

15. Crimp the flap along the existing creases.

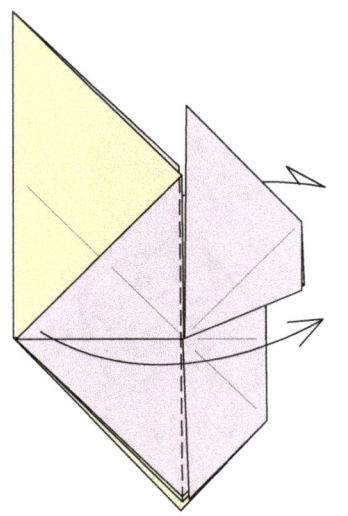

16. Swing a flap over at each side.

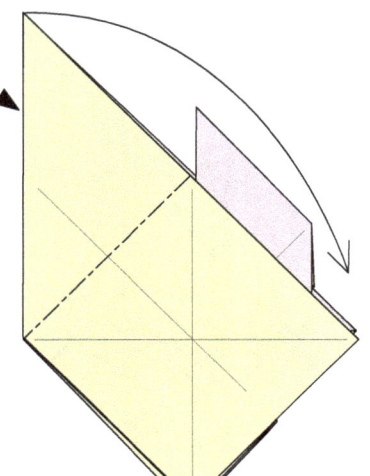

17. Reverse fold the flap though.

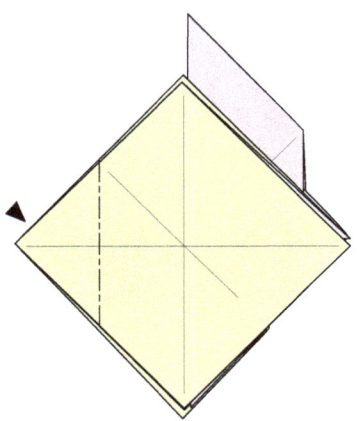

18. Sink the corner halfway.

octopus

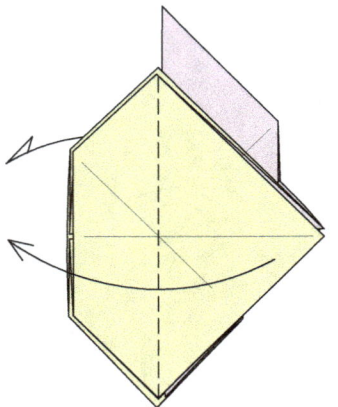

19. Swing the side flaps back over.

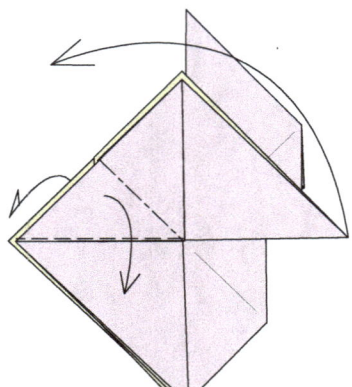

20. Crimp the flap up.

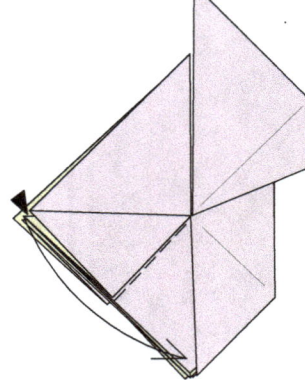

21. Reverse fold the hidden flap through.

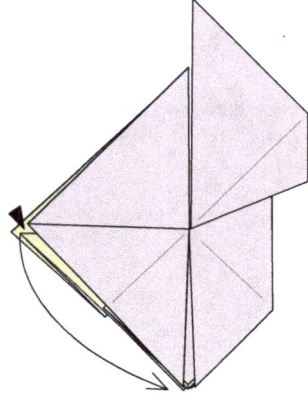

22. Reverse fold the hidden flap through on the other side.

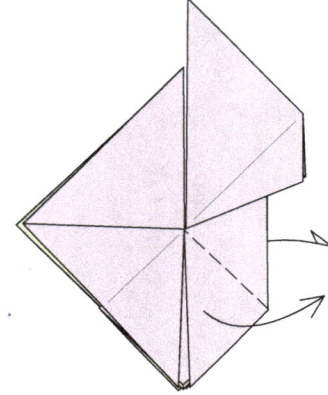

23. Swing a flap over at each side.

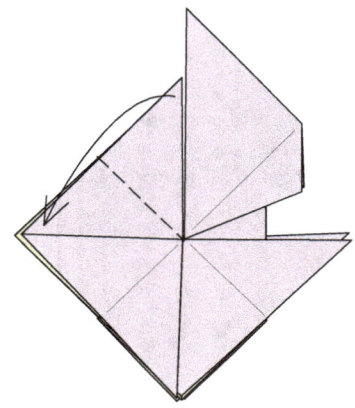

24. Valley fold the corner over.

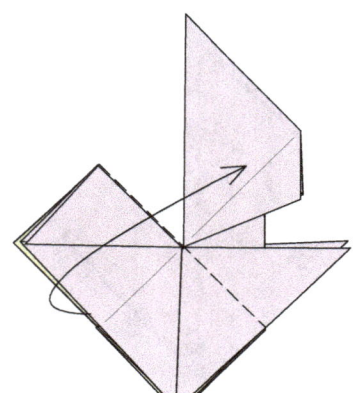

25. Open out the top layers, revealing the sunken flap.

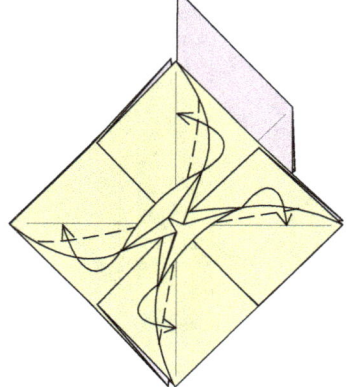

26. Flatten out the center flap by valley folding the corners to the creases.

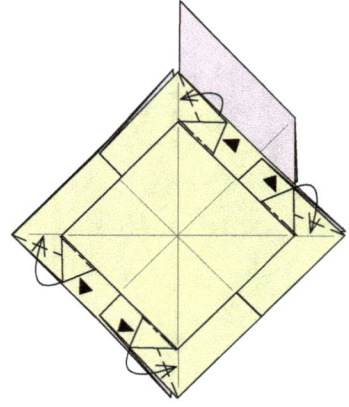

27. Reverse fold the four corners.

octopus

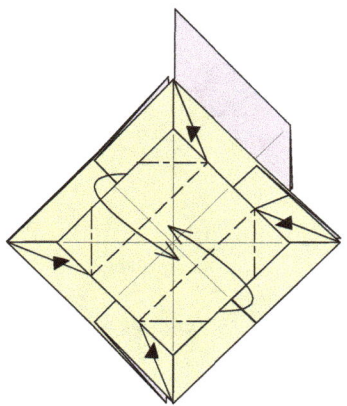
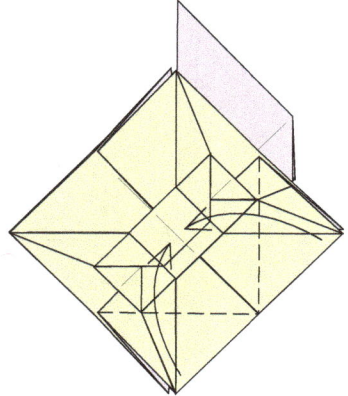
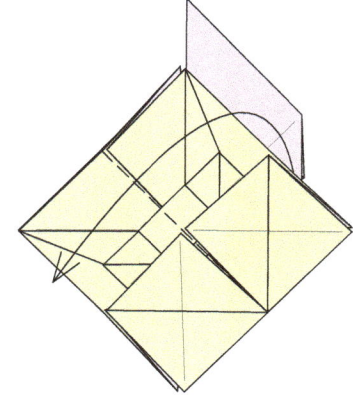

28. Valley fold the edges over while squash folding the corners. The flaps will overlap slightly.

29. Valley fold the top corners to the center.

30. Valley fold in half.

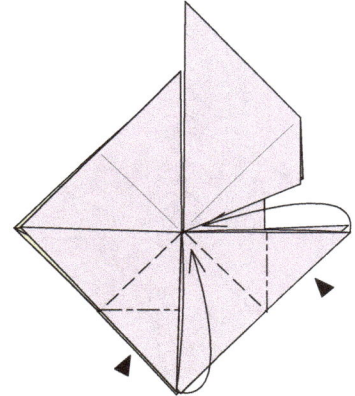
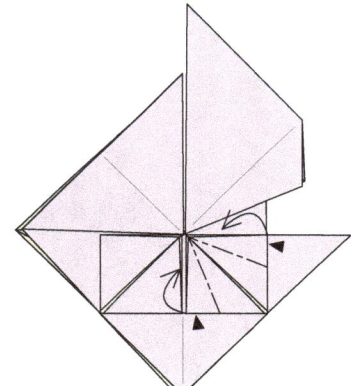
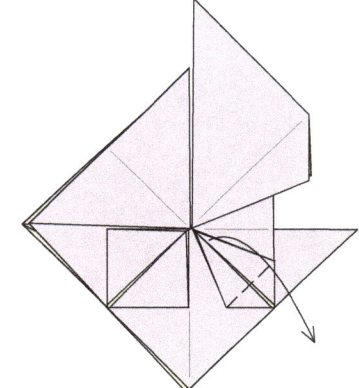

31. Squash fold the two corners.

32. Reverse fold the sides.

33. Valley fold the flap down.

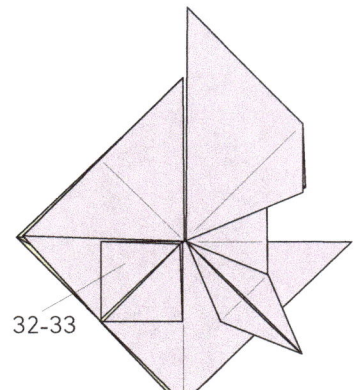
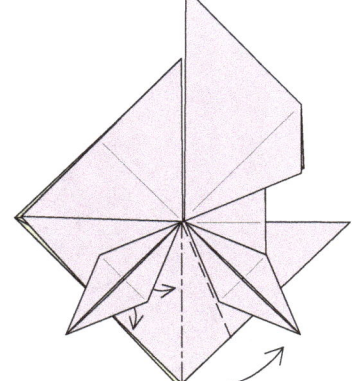
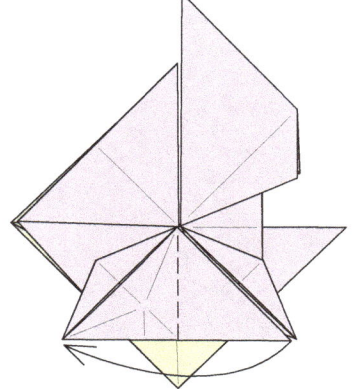

34. Repeat steps 32-33 on the other flap.

35. Pull the top single layer over, releasing the trapped layers.

36. Pull the flap in the other direction, releasing the layers from the other side.

octopus

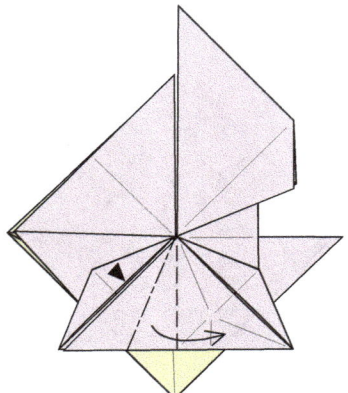

37. Squash fold the flap down.

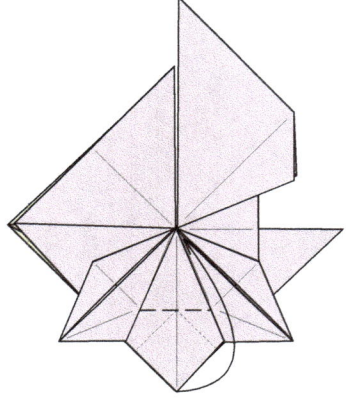

38. Valley fold the flap up, allowing the middle layers to squash fold.

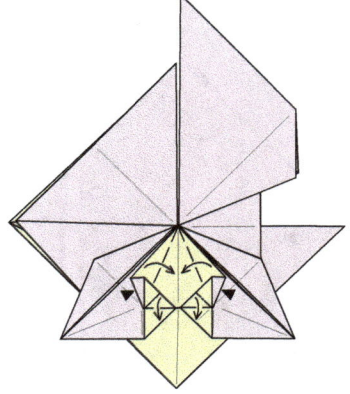

39. Valley fold the sides to the center, swivel folding down at the base of the flap.

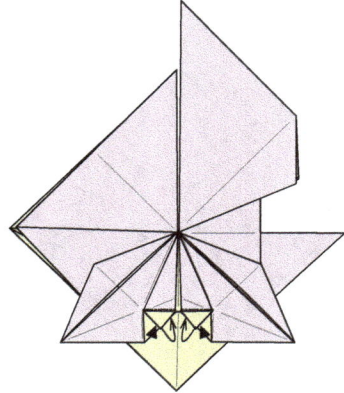

40. Reverse fold the corners inside.

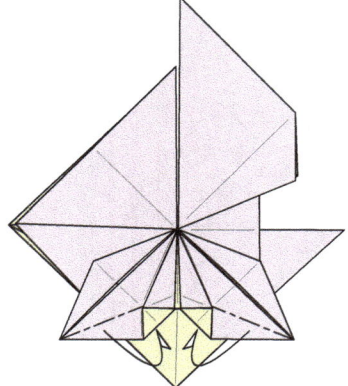

41. Mountain fold the edges inside. They should *not* wrap around any layers.

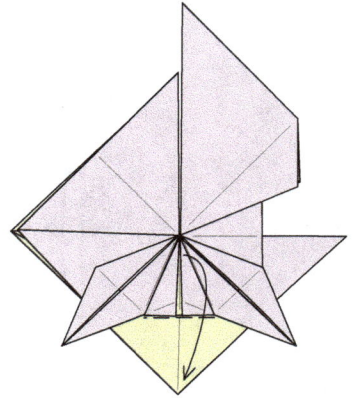

42. Swing the flap down.

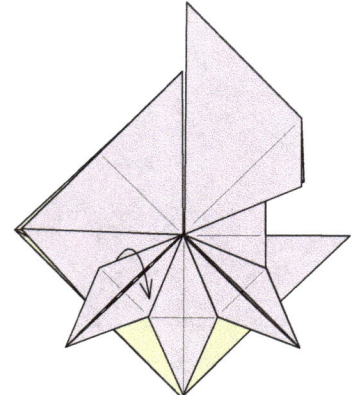

43. Valley fold the flap in half.

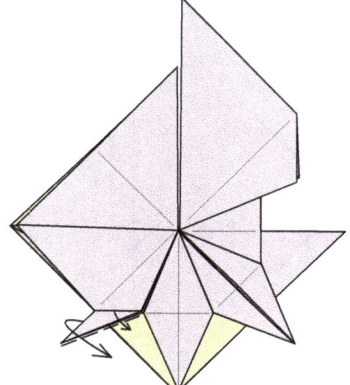

44. Pull out the top single layer and flatten.

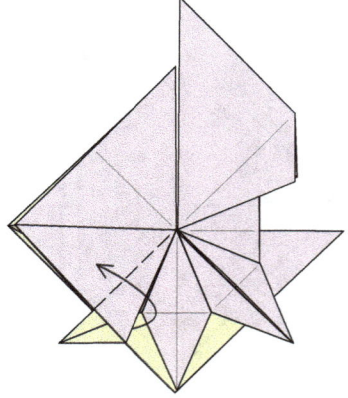

45. Swing the flap back over.

octopus

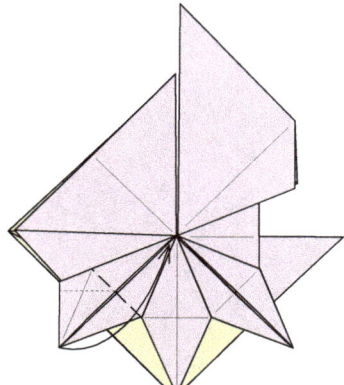
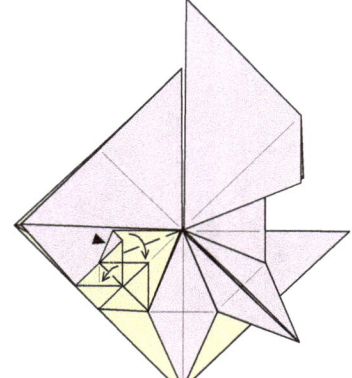
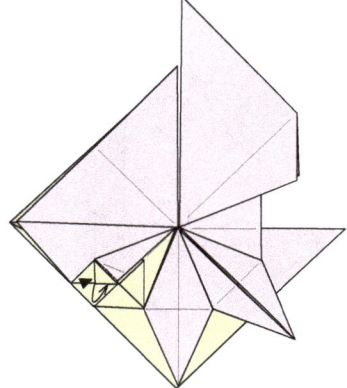

46. Valley fold the flap up, allowing the middle layer to squash fold.

47. Valley fold the side to the center, swivel folding down at the base of the flap.

48. Reverse fold the corner inside.

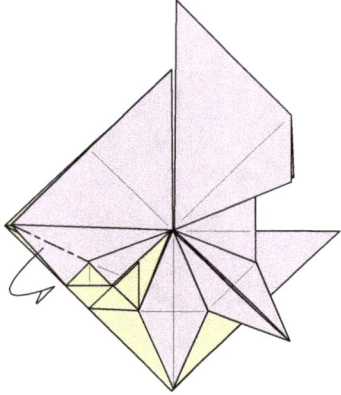
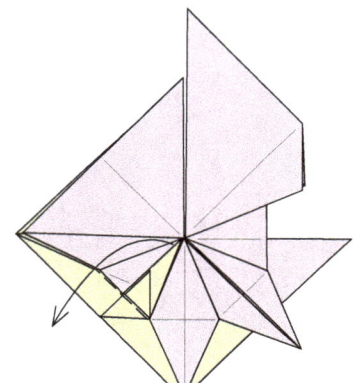
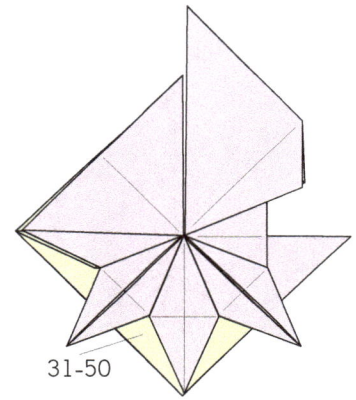

49. Mountain fold the edge inside. It should *not* wrap around any layers.

50. Swing the flap outwards.

51. Repeat steps 31-50 behind.

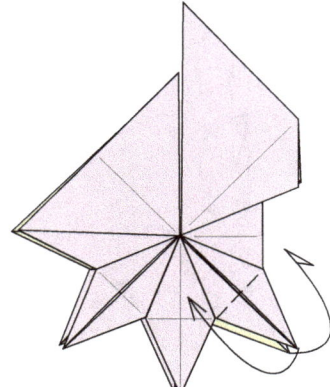
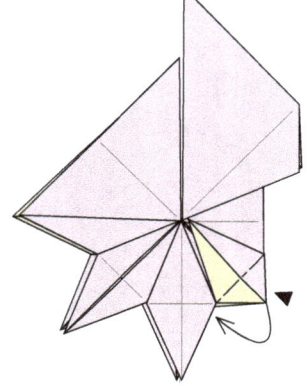
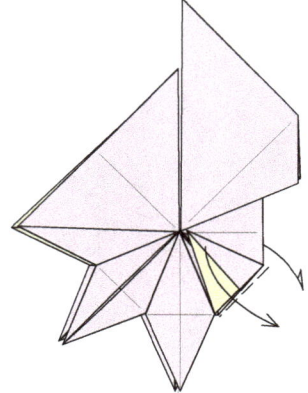

52. Valley fold a flap up at each side.

53. Reverse fold the corner.

54. Swing the side flaps back down.

121

octopus

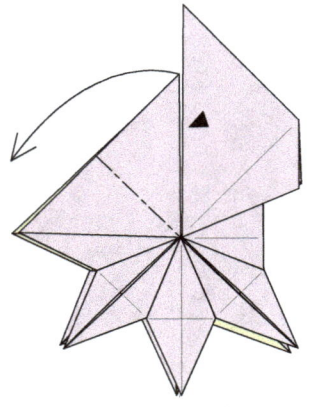

55. Reverse fold the flap over.

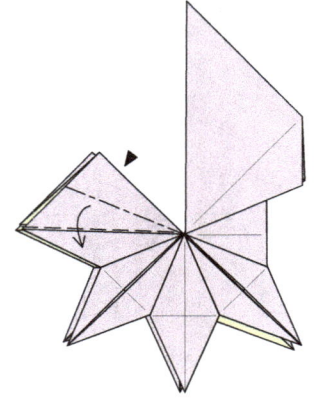

56. Squash fold the top flap.

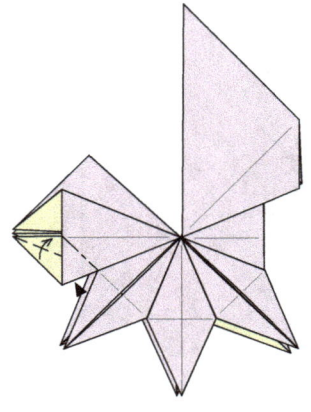

57. Reverse fold the bottom section.

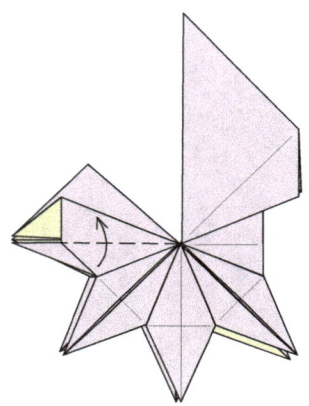

58. Swing the flap up.

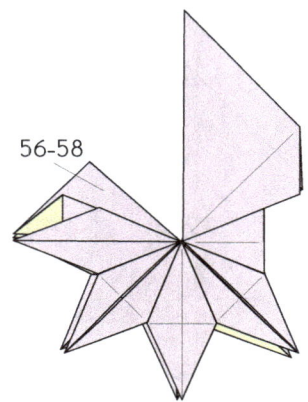

59. Repeat steps 56-58 behind.

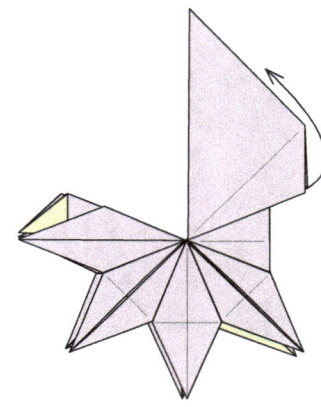

60. Swing the small flap at the rear upwards.

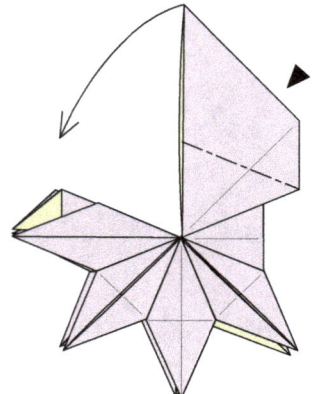

61. Spread squash the large flap.

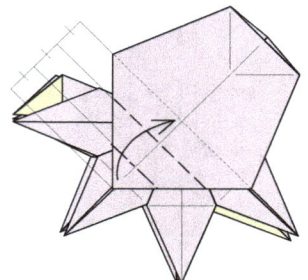

62. Pleat the tip of the flap into thirds.

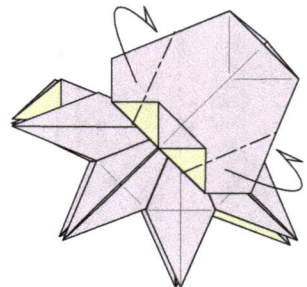

63. Mountain fold the sides of the flap as desired.

octopus

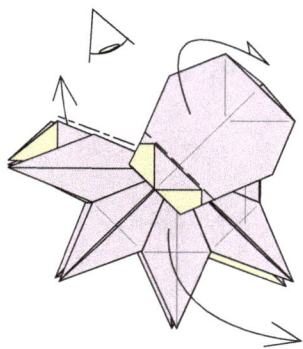 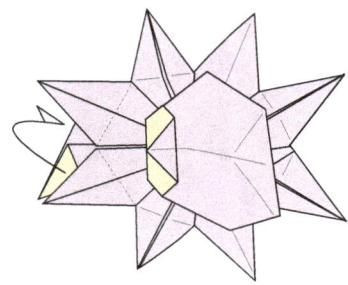 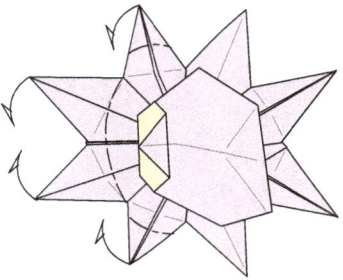

64. Spread apart the model along the center. The base will not flatten completely. Rotate the head flap allowing the colored eyes to rest on the base.

65. View from previous step. Mountain fold the center flap as far as possible, locking the legs together.

66. Curl the front sets of legs down so the model tilts upwards.

67. Completed *Octopus*.